I'm Sorry

Repairing a Hurtful Relationship

Jay Krunszyinsky

I'm Sorry

Repairing a Hurtful Relationship

Jay Krunszyinsky

Word Association Publishers
205 Fifth Avenue
Tarentum, Pennsylvania 15084

Printed in the United States of America.

ISBN: 1-932205-02-0
Library of Congress Control Number: 2002114672

Word Association Publishers
205 Fifth Avenue,
Tarentum, Pennsylvania 15084

www.wordassociation.com

CONTENTS

ACKNOWLEDGEMENTS

I would like to extend my sincere thanks to my wife, Barbara, for her never-ending patience and support, not only during the writing of this book, but also each day in our relationship. She truly exemplifies the virtues of love, respect, and honesty that are presented in this book. She has been my inspiration and my best friend. I am so very blessed to be loved by her and our two children, Rachel and Molly. I am sorry that my writing this book has taken precious time away from each of them. I love all of them very much.

I would also like to acknowledge my parents for ensuring that I developed a morality based on teachings of absolute standards of right and wrong. I will always love and respect both of them. I appreciate the love and encouragement that they both gave me throughout my life. I thank them for the home-cooked meals, the gifts of money, the encouraging words, and the other acts of respect and love that they both continue to show. My sisters, Vicky, Kim, and Chris, also need to be mentioned here since they were very instrumental in my development as a child. My sisters were very interested in me as a brother and as a human being and have continued to love and respect me throughout my adulthood. I am very fortunate to have siblings who do care.

Last, I would like to acknowledge my editors, Nan Newell and Karen Hadley, for their abilities to bring to life the very important messages in this book during a time when rational thoughts need to prevail in our country. This message is clearer and better because of your work. Between the three of us, we have a final product that should inspire and help others to get back to those virtues that represent the foundation of every meaningful relationship.

INTRODUCTION

You come home from work each day and just want to be left alone. You are tired of hearing how hurtful you are. All you want to do is to gather your thoughts. You will never get to those things that need to get done. You never get the opportunities to have fun like you had in the past. You always have to be the responsible person in the relationship and make sure everything gets done the right way. Every time you point out how others can be more responsible, you are ignored or told you are a bad communicator. All right, sometimes you raise your voice and make harsh statements that you don't mean. You just want the other person in your relationship to understand the pressures you are under. What does this person want from you? Is asking this person to take care of his or her responsibilities asking too much?

You want to feel good and enjoy the same pleasures of life that you see depicted on television and in the movies. You see other people enjoying this life. They are going to parties, meeting new people, and getting what they want when they want it. You wonder what is preventing you from improving your life along with your relationship—a relationship that seems to be more and more damaged as time goes on.

Your thoughts are not as uncommon as you may think. You have developed beliefs and thoughts that have contributed to your negative feelings about your relationship. What you will learn in the next chapter is how thoughts influence feelings and behavior. For example, your positive thoughts will induce happy feelings and prompt you to act in positive ways. Your negative thoughts will cause you to feel and act in negative ways. You have been bombarded with messages in the media, at school, at work, and in your community that you need to take good care of yourself and enjoy life. The glamorization of wealth, sex, alcohol, and instant gratification has influenced your thinking. What is wrong with your wanting wealth, sex, alcohol, and the instant pleasures of life? You most likely have experienced some of these symbols of enjoyment in your life. How happy were you during these experiences? Have you experienced an empty feeling at some point while you were engaged in fun and frolicking? You may find that there have not been many times you have experienced sustained joy or happiness in a relationship. You may have participated in relationships that were grounded in the themes of alcohol, sex, or material wealth. Even today you may continue to feel the way you did then, and you hear the same messages that you were hurtful and you were unable to communicate.

As you read through this book, you will be challenged to look at the kinds of thought processes that you use to evaluate your relationship. You will also be challenged to evaluate your behavior in your relationship to determine if it is hurtful. You will be given ideas as to how to enhance your relationship through meaningful acts. Through this process, you may discover that your present thoughts are not rational and that you are misperceiving the actions of the other person in the relationship. When you learn how to develop a rational approach to evaluating behavior in your relationship, you will discover new priorities in your life.

Once you begin to see the hurt you are causing, you will understand the importance of atoning. The act of saying you are sorry may sound meaningless to you at this time. If you say you're sorry before you shift to more meaningful behaviors in your relationship, you will not convince the other person that you are genuinely sorry. Through your development of meaningful relationship skills, you will start to understand the power of atoning for the hurt that you cause. When you begin to connect with the other person in your relationship, your apology will be heartfelt, and you and the other person will experience an uplifting and deepened connection.

You may be convinced that you are the one who is owed an apology. You are the one who is struggling to get out of bed and face each day. You have been the one who attempts to provide a perfect life for the two of you. You just might be so consumed with stress, worry, and apprehension that you need more from the other person in your relationship. Have you ever asked the other person what he or she wants from you? You may be surprised by the answer, for you may believe that you have been providing for these needs. After reading this book, you will see where you have fallen short of the mark and how you can improve. Once both of you get a common vision through a shared system of meaningful behavior, you both will adopt more realistic priorities for your relationship.

Are you ready to look at a new way of repairing your relationship, one that has never been shown to you? Pay special attention to the term *morality* throughout this book. This has been viewed as a taboo concept today. In the next chapter, you will learn about a modified version of morality that allows for less meaning in a relationship. It is called relativism. You most likely have allowed this new version to guide your thoughts, feelings, and actions. This and other factors may be causing you to see the world and your relationship in irrational ways.

One

LET'S BE RATIONAL

Are you a rational or irrational thinker? You may want to believe you are a rational thinker, but you find that you are the eternal pessimist, able to see only the half-empty glass in many situations you face. You are a rational thinker if you turn negative situations into positive ones. You can face unpleasant situations and not become overwhelmed. You use your unique talents to resolve problems and view the brighter side of your life. If you are an irrational thinker, you will either overreact to problems or will not react at all. You will experience intense emotional pain when challenged to take responsibility for your actions or to acknowledge how your action may negatively impact another person. You become easily overwhelmed by the pace of work, family, and community responsibilities. You see negative qualities in the other person in your relationship and react in subtle ways to hurt him or her.

You have an internal monologue that runs through your day. Thoughts that are self-defeating or that provide unrealistic expectations for you are irrational thoughts. Using words like *always, have to,* and *never* can make thoughts irrational and expectations unrealistic. Thoughts that produce second-guessing messages such as "would have," "should have," and "could have" are irrational. By focusing your energy on thoughts that will not resolve problems or engage others in the here-and-now, you can send subtle, hurtful messages to another person. Thoughts that are uplifting and provide you with real solutions to everyday problems are rational thoughts. Rational thoughts will not always provide you with a warm, fuzzy feeling, but they will allow you to see the possibilities to get through the challenges of life. Rational thoughts help you to keep your perspective and priorities grounded in the truth. When you begin to feel that your life is awful and there is no hope, you are thinking irrationally.

Did you know that your thinking will influence how you feel and behave? Your thoughts are the guiding force behind your total social presentation. When you think rationally, you will experience positive feelings and demonstrate positive behavior. You will be more apt to act responsibly because you will see the situation much more clearly and feel more positive that you are doing the right thing for the other person. When you look at your relationship in a rational way, you take the time to assess how you are positively or negatively impacting the other person. You will see the unique qualities of the other person in your relationship. You will value the person's thoughts and feelings and allow this person to demonstrate his or her talents. You will not place conditions on your love, and you will engage in an open and honest dialogue.

Instead, you may be causing the shame, anger, and guilt in the other person in your relationship. You may be the source of the resentment or even the hate. If you are involved in an unhappy relationship, you may be acting and feeling in negative ways that are guided by your irrational thinking. If so, you would benefit from knowing the factors that contribute to your irrational thinking. There are three areas in which these factors may have surfaced during your life. They are your psychiatric or developmental stability, your childhood family setting, and your childhood school setting.

MENTAL ILLNESS AND IRRATIONALITY

Did you know that one out of every three people suffers from a mental illness? Do you struggle with panic attacks, social fears, emptiness, paranoid thoughts, or extreme highs and lows? As a child, did you grow up with anxiety, attention problems, depression, social interaction problems, developmental problems, extreme energy, or involuntary vocal or motor tics? Did you find yourself pushing others away when you really wanted them to get close to you? The important factor to remember is that many of these disorders cause the person to think irrationally and to hurt others in his relationships. Many times, people with psychiatric and developmental problems do not intend to hurt, nor do they recognize the hurt they cause.

You may be wondering what types of irrational thoughts can prevent a person suffering a mental or developmental disorder from gaining insight into the hurt that he may cause another person. Major depression is a very prevalent psychiatric illness in society and will serve as a good example. Do you know what thoughts, feelings, and actions are associated with this disorder? The *Diagnostic and Statistical Manual of Mental Disorders, Fourth Edition* (DSM-IV) is the manual used to classify mental and developmental disorders. The DSM-IV categorizes the thoughts of a depressed person as irrational. A depressed person thinks that there is no way to solve his problems or to change his life circumstances. This is why a depressed person may have recurrent thoughts of death and suicide. His thoughts produce feelings of sadness, emptiness, fearfulness, worthlessness, and guilt. Some of the behaviors associated with depression include insomnia, diminished interest or pleasure in almost all activities, significant weight loss, and loss of energy each day. A person who possesses these thoughts, feelings, and behaviors will hurt other people in his relationships, though many times he will not recognize that he is doing so. This person will not communicate his problem with another person in a rational manner, nor will he look for ways to resolve his conflicts. This causes the other people in his relationships to also feel overwhelmed, helpless, and frustrated.

Many of the other psychiatric and developmental problems outlined in the DSM-IV involve irrational thoughts. People with schizophrenia experience delusions, or false beliefs. These beliefs, which are the results of their auditory and visual hallucinations, can range from paranoid thoughts that people are attempting to harm them to beliefs that they have special powers and abilities not based in reality. Some adults and children with hyperactivity or mania think that their activities should provide constant stimulation and pleasure. They place their priorities on people, places, and events that are stimulating to them, which causes them to become disorganized and lose focus. People with various addictions obsessively think about their addicting activity. Many people with personality disorders do not think that others value or love them. They spend much of their time finding ways to make their irrational thoughts become self-fulfilling prophecies. Through their irrational belief that they are not valued or loved, they treat others poorly and set expectations that cannot be met for the other people in their relationships. The antisocial person believes that he should be able to satisfy his needs and wants regardless of the social norms and laws of society.

TRAUMA

Psychiatric illnesses can occur as a result of trauma. Have you ever suffered a traumatic event in your life? People who suffer traumatic life events such as abuse, disaster, abduction, or the ravages of war can also adopt irrational thought processes due to the trauma they experience. This also includes individuals who witness horrific acts such as murder and abuse. Many people who experience trauma also suffer from Posttraumatic Stress Disorder. Many times they avoid activities, people, and places in their environment that remind them of their trauma. They are consumed with thoughts that the traumatic event will occur again. Their irrational thoughts cause strain on their relationships, many times causing the severance of those relationships. They often lose the ability to gauge who they can or cannot trust. They may either demand too much control of the other person in a relationship or become too passive. This causes them to behave in unpredictable ways in relationships. Many times, children who suffer trauma also have a caretaker who acts in ways that further confuse them and reinforce irrational thoughts and fears.

Raquel was a five-year-old girl who lived with her maternal grandmother. Raquel had been brutally beaten and raped by her mother's boyfriend when she was four years old. Raquel was receiving family counseling to help her and her grandmother work through this traumatic situation. The family counselor discovered how much Raquel loved one of the cups in the kitchen cabinet. It was an old cup that had the face of Santa Claus on it. The grandmother was outraged at the suggestion that Raquel be given milk in this cup before bedtime. This would mean more work for her and was out of the question. The grandmother also shared her displeasure with the counselor's suggestion that

Raquel be read a story each night before bed. The grandmother stated that she needed her time each night and did not have the time for this.

Medication can help many individuals who suffer from mental and developmental disabilities from acting in aggressive or bizarre ways. Even so, irrational thinking will continue for many people with disabilities. Medications will not address their need to function in social situations, which contributes to the losses that they experience in their relationships. Many become so absorbed by their irrational thoughts that they fail to recognize how their behavior hurts others. This hurt can be subtle in nature and consist of selfishness, disrespect, and dishonesty. The person with the psychiatric problem may demonstrate the need to have others support him, but he does not reciprocate supportive behavior. With irrational thoughts guiding his feelings and behavior, the person with a psychiatric problem will not take the initiative to notice the redeeming qualities of another person and show love. As we saw in the example involving Raquel, a family setting may involve factors that contribute to or reinforce a person's irrational thought processes.

NEGATIVE MESSAGES

How did your experiences with a parent contribute to your way of thinking today? Some people receive many negative messages throughout their childhood. Those who received negative messages as children develop irrational thought processes that carry over into their adult life. Edmund J. Bourne, Ph.D. wrote about the childhood origins of anxiety disorders in his book, *The Anxiety & Phobia Workbook.* He postulated that children who grow up with critical parents who are perfectionists will experience self-doubt about whether they are "good enough" or are "sufficiently worthy." He reported that these children grow up feeling insecure and become dependent on safety. Many of these children grow up to become perfectionists later in life. Are you driving yourself or another person to be perfect in your relationship? The high expectation of perfection is irrational for anyone in a relationship. Can you be perfect? You live in a world that reinforces high standards and achievement. Can your relationship work with this same philosophy? The perfectionist contributes to the hurt in a relationship through critical statements and blame. A person's critical behaviors represent another subtle kind of hurt in a relationship, which can go unrecognized by the criticizer.

Alanis Morissette's song, "Perfect," depicts the irrational thoughts of perfectionists.

> Sometimes is never quite enough
> If you're flawless, then you'll win my love
> Don't forget to win first place
> Don't forget to keep that smile on your face
> Be a good boy
> Try a little harder
> You've got to measure up
> And make me prouder
> How long before you screw it up
> How many times do I have to tell you to hurry up
> With everything I do for you
> The least you can do is keep quiet
> Be a good girl

You've gotta try a little harder
That simply wasn't good enough
To make us proud
I'll live through you
I'll make you what I never was
If you're the best, then maybe so am I
Compared to him compared to her
I'm doing this for your own damn good
You'll make up for what I blew
What's the problem... why are you crying
Be a good boy
Push a little farther now
That wasn't fast enough
To make us happy
We'll love you just the way you are if you're perfect

Other negative messages may consist of the child not feeling loved and respected. Can you remember the times you were made to feel hated or disrespected by a parent? Did a parent consistently lie to you? Did your parent have a favorite child? Were you blamed for your parents' problems in their marriage? Did you think you were the cause of a parent's hate or disrespect toward you?

Burt and Cynthia have been married for twenty years and have four children: Burt Jr., age seventeen; Judy, age fourteen; Jonathan, age nine; and Becky, age four. Burt and Cynthia have experienced some marital problems recently. Cynthia's mother, Marge, has baby-sat the younger children and has been pointing out to the children how their father has not been spending enough time with them. Marge has also pointed this out to Cynthia and has told Cynthia that Burt is just like her father. Burt Jr. cannot stand his maternal grandmother and tells his father the bad things she is telling the other children. Burt Sr. takes out his frustration on the three younger children and tells them that they are rotten kids and that they are never satisfied. He threatens that someday he will leave them with their mother to survive on their own with no help from him. Burt and Cynthia argue frequently in front of the children and threaten to leave one another.

Does this happen in real life? How irrational do you think some children will become when exposed to negative messages from parents?

On October 1, 1997, high school student Luke Woodham opened fire on several students in Pearl High School in Pearl, Washington. He killed two of the students and wounded seven. He began his day by slitting his mother's throat before he headed to school in her car with a rifle tucked underneath a trench coat. Luke talked to one of the students he wounded and apologized, claiming he was not shooting at anyone in particular. Police Chief Bill Slade said Luke had written a detailed note, saying he felt he'd been wronged and that he killed because people like him are mistreated every day. During his 1998 trial for killing his mother, Luke stated he killed his mother because "she always never loved me." He went on to state that his mother blamed him for her divorce and problems with his brother. He also stated that his mother spent much time away from home. Luke wrote about how he and an accomplice beat his dog, Sparkle, then set it on fire and threw it in a pond. He wrote, "I hit her so hard I knocked the fur off her neck. It was true beauty."

If you believed your parents' negative messages as a child, you grew up with irrational thoughts that have influenced your thought processes. Due to your irrational beliefs, your actions toward someone in a present relationship may not be based on reality. Do you find yourself overreacting to comments made by a person in your relationship? Do you automatically interpret someone's critical feedback as an expression of hate or rejection? How would you respond to someone you thought hated you or was rejecting you? In these instances, many people either avoid the problem or become very aggressive. In either case, the person's behavior resulting from his irrational beliefs from the past would contribute to his hurtful acts in a present relationship. The problem is that he will not always recognize his actions as hurtful. Many people who receive negative messages as children enter relationships as adults sending similar messages.

Codependency and the Enabler

When you were a child, did you grow up in a home where your parents or caretakers took little to no responsibility for their problems or behaviors? Did you witness a parent support the behavior of the other regardless of how destructive it was? A parent providing this support was an enabler. A parent bases his or her enabling on manipulation and dishonesty that hurts others in subtle ways. Children are robbed of their ability to see a relationship clearly due to the inconsistent messages of the enabling parent. Children are also reinforced for depending heavily on their codependent parent, which robs them of their own development in decision-making.

Angela Miller wrote about the enabler:

When not in check,

I will:
Pick up your shoes
Carry your pack
Pay your traffic ticket
Lie to your boss
Do your homework
Remove rocks from your path
And strip you of the joy
Of saying, "I did it myself!"

Do you possess codependent traits? Codependent personalities evolve from attempts to keep some type of order in a hurtful relationship. The term *codependency* refers to a relationship where one or both parties enable the other to act in certain maladaptive ways. Many times, the act of enabling satisfies a need for the codependent person because his or her actions foster a dependency from the other person or persons in the relationship. Did your family have an alcoholic or drug-dependent parent? To enable the parent with the addiction, the codependent parent makes excuses and lies for the addict, which enables the addiction to continue. Codependency is reinforced by a person's need to be needed.

The enabler thinks irrationally by believing he can maintain healthy relationships through manipulation and control. He believes he can do this by avoiding conflict and fostering dependency. Is it rational for someone to think that he can maintain a healthy relationship when he does not address problems and he lies to protect others from their responsibilities? The way a codependent person can continue to foster this dependency from others is by controlling situations and people around him. As a child, you may have been reinforced to comply with actions and decisions of a parent instead of being afforded opportunities to challenge those actions that you found to be wrong. Can you see how these types of messages could foster the development of irrational thinking? The ongoing themes in a codependent home are to avoid conflicts and problems and to make excuses for destructive or hurtful behavior.

Scott is a seventeen-year-old boy who knew that he needed to be by his mother's side in order to protect her from his father. His mother told him how much she loved him and needed him. Scott was a well-built boy who was popular in school. Many of the girls in his class liked him. He grew fond of one of the girls and asked her out on a date. Scott's mother did not approve of him going out with the girl. She went to his father and stated that he needed to do something about his boy who wanted to have sex with girls. Scott and his father got into a physical confrontation, resulting in Scott having to go to the hospital to get a cast put on his broken arm. Scott could not understand why his mother lied when the doctor asked how his arm was broken. Scott and his mother's relationship improved once he stopped dating.

Can you relate to Scott? Over time, children develop a dependency on their codependent parent to help them through their life. Their codependent parent's need to be needed makes this relationship dysfunctional and filled with hurt. In many instances, hurt can result from the codependent parent's attempts to keep the peace in the family. Over time, the only way a codependent parent can accomplish this is by being manipulative and controlling of relationships. He often controls these relationships by provoking the abusive parent to carry out undeserved punitive action to further promote the child's dependency on the codependent parent.

Why does enabling cause so much hurt in a relationship? What is the harm with trying to keep the peace? Part of this was answered in the previous example. The power afforded to the codependent person in a relationship reinforces his need for control even if he uses inappropriate means to fulfill his need to be in control. A second and overlooked reason centers on the inconsistent messages and unclear expectations presented by someone who is codependent. These characteristics contribute to a relationship filled with irrational thoughts and behavior. This kind of relationship has no clear rules to right and wrong behavior.

There are circumstances within a family's composition that leads a parent to act in irrational ways. This, in turn, can contribute to the child's irrational thought processes. Did you know that close to sixty percent of families were headed by a single parent in 1994? Did you also know that 75 percent of families with children had both parents working? These numbers demonstrate the various roles and challenges parents take on today. Did your parents take on job and social roles that took their attention away from you? Many parents are forced to work because of the costs to raise a family. In some families, both parents work in the pursuit of more material wealth. Each endeavor is admirable as long as the family is grounded in a morality that places importance on the relationships within the family unit. A child who experiences rejection from his parent due to these factors will make attempts to redirect the parent's attention. If this fails, the child will find other means to meet his needs, many times acting in maladaptive ways to cope with the stress in his life. He may demonstrate addictive behavior, social withdrawal, or even violence.

THE "FEEL-GOOD" MORALITY

Televisions, stereos, computers, video games, and friends are means by which children develop their sense of right and wrong in many families. Do you think children should develop their own sense of morality from means outside of their parents? In the hustle and bustle of life, a parent might be more apt to allow his child to turn to one of these mediums for extended periods of time. This does not allow a child to develop clear expectations of what constitutes right and wrong behavior. This also leaves the child to determine right and wrong by the social customs to which he is exposed. Have you ever heard the term *moral relativism*? Moral relativism means that moral standards are grounded only in social custom. Morals are defined as good acts. Do you know how you can get a good act to remain good if the social custom is hurtful? Don't worry, I do not know the answer either. The terms moral and relativism are contradictory. The prevailing thought or custom of society needs to contain a safeguard to prevent immorality. How will you keep your behavior in check if you do not adopt a morality that contains absolute rights and wrongs?

Today, more and more children are adopting their parents' "feel good" morality, which often causes them to inflict hurt toward others. If more people declare a behavior an acceptable social custom, the behavior will become morally acceptable according to a relative moral view. A person's view on a social custom can be influenced by music, television, movies, literature, and societal trends. If these views are not held to a standard that is absolute in regards to right and wrong behavior, the person can begin to lose his ability to see the line between good and bad.

Have you ever searched for a good feeling through sex, drugs, material possessions, or open expressions of anger or rage? Are your thoughts rational when you think that you can maintain a healthy relationship while pursuing only those things that make you feel good? What is right or wrong without having an absolute morality? You may question how this absolute standard is set. This will be defined and explained in more detail in the next chapter.

Susan is a seventeen-year-old growing up in a family that does not teach morality. Susan and her friends have classroom discussions with teachers and counselors saying that sexual activity is appropriate if both people are consenting and safe sex is practiced. Through the media and discussions with other students, Susan concludes that the act of oral sex is not considered sexual due to this act not involving penetration. Susan really loves her boyfriend and decides this is a way to remain a virgin and show her boyfriend she loves him.

Can you relate to Susan or Susan's parents in this example? If you have watched the news and special reports on television, you have been informed that this example has occurred among many teenagers. Many boys and girls believe they are keeping their virginity by engaging in oral sex. They perceive the social custom to be that oral sex is not sex. Where have you heard this before? This is an another example of moral relativism. The conclusion made by Susan was not based on rational thought processes. If Susan understood that her actions were in direct opposition to an absolute moral code that defines acts of love and intimacy, she would make more rational choices. If her parents developed clear behavioral expectations based upon specific virtues, she would be faced with the responsibility of making a decision either to respect her parents' view on morality or not. This is not to say that Susan would not have engaged in a sexual relationship. Her choice needed to be based upon her knowing that this behavior had consequences and was not endorsed by her parents or the other systems of care in her life. She and her boyfriend would need to learn what virtues should guide their decisions, and develop behavior expectations based upon these virtues. These expectations would need to align with their parents' expectations in these same areas. Her thought that oral sex was not sex was easily adopted, since she did not have an absolute morality to challenge this view. As you see, irrational thoughts can be used to justify behavior and avoid responsibility. The person who thinks in morally relative terms would experience difficulties recognizing the hurt that he would cause another person.

The abuse that children suffer within their families also contributes to their irrational thinking. Do you see how the thoughts and actions of parents can contribute to their children's adopting the same thoughts and behavior patterns? More than three children die each day as a result of child abuse in the home. In 1998, approximately 1100 children died of abuse and neglect. Most of the children who die are under the age of 5; 38 percent of the children are under the age of 1. This is the leading cause of death for infants and young children. This includes falls, choking on food, suffocation, drowning, residential fires, and motor vehicle accidents. Almost one-half of all substantiated cases of neglect and abuse in a family are associated with a parent's alcohol or drug abuse. As mentioned previously, people with addictions are grounded in irrational thoughts.

Children can act in horrific ways because of the irrational thoughts they develop from negative verbal messages, sexual and physical abuse, and moral relativism.

Brendan Smith was sixteen years old when she killed two people and injured nine. She had decided to shoot a 22-caliber rifle across the street from her house onto the entrance of Grover Cleveland Elementary School in San Diego, California, on January 29, 1979. She discussed how her violence grew out of an abusive home. She claimed that her father beat and sexually abused her for years. She stated, "I had to share my dad's bed 'til I was fourteen years old." She went on to say that her father bought her a gun for Christmas when she asked for a radio. Brendan was the original school rampager.

On September 2, 1996, fourteen-year-old Barry Loukaitis broke into algebra class at the Frontier Junior High School in Moses Lake, Washington, with a high-powered rifle and shot three students and their teacher. Two of the students and the teacher died. Students recalled that Barry shot one of the students with whom he was always having a conflict. Barry's mother suspected that one of the songs that Barry listened to had driven him to commit the crime. The father suggested that the family had three generations' worth of depressive illnesses in the family. Barry's mother told the jury that she treated her son as a "confidant" and told him everything. She went on to say that this included plans to kill herself in front of her ex-husband and his girlfriend on Valentine's Day, 1996. He had been an honor student at school.

The hurt in families is being broadcast in the media more and more. The media is also endorsing acts of abuse. Do you know that there are people in academia who endorse pedophilia? In the April 22, 2002, edition of *U.S. News & World Report,* John Leo wrote an article entitled, "Apologists for pedophilia." Larry Constantine, a Massachusetts family therapist and sex book writer, stated that children "have the right to express themselves sexually, which means they may or may not have contact with people older than themselves." Wardell Pomeroy, coauthor of the original Kinsey reports, stated that incest "can be sometimes beneficial." Minnesota sociologists included pedophile sex with those "intimate relations that are important and precious."

There are propedophilia rationalizations still being made today. Some of these rationalizations include the following statements: "Children are sexual beings with the right to pick their partners." "The quality of relationships, not age, determines the value of sex." "Most pedophiles are gentle and harmless." "The damage of pedophilia comes mostly from the shocked horror communicated by parents, not the sex itself." A new controversial book called *Harmful to Minors: The Perils of Protecting Children from Sex* by author Judith Levine, contains a foreword by former Surgeon General Joycelyn Elders. One report said that this book plays down the dangers of pedophilia and that Levine thinks this is a good time to endorse "some priest-boy sex." The report discussed how the "disorder of the intellectual world" trickles into the popular culture, including the school system. Tom O'Carrol has been asked to address the international sex convention in Paris regarding the private rights of pedophiles and their children partners. His pedophile book is on a course list at Cambridge University. If more people in society find this to be acceptable behavior, pedophilia will be a morally acceptable behavior. Does this sound like rational thinking to you?

Do you think that a public school setting influences a child's irrational thinking? You spent close to seven hours a day, 180 days a year for twelve years in a learning institution. Many of your social and learning skills were developed and acted out in these institutions for over twelve years. Many teachers indirectly help children to develop problem-solving skills and other social skills. They set up positive reinforcement programs that help children to develop positive engagement and problem resolution skills. Public school systems refrain from incorporating a program that teaches and upholds a moral code surrounding behaviors considered virtuous. Public schools receive public funding, and school administrators are resistant to incorporate any program that would depict any system of moral absolutes or good versus bad behavior for fear they will lose federal funding. Instead, the school setting is an environment where students are exposed to negative messages from other students and find comfort in moral relativism, especially if they have no other means to process their thoughts. You already know how relativistic views contribute to a person's irrational thinking.

Johnny is a fourth-grade student who is involved in a school project to create a drama that depicts the plotting of a murder in such a manner that the murderer gets away with his or her actions. Johnny is told that his final grade is based upon his ability to critically think about all the possible evidence trails he could leave and to be able to cover his tracks leaving no evidence. To make this task easier for Johnny, the teacher allows him to use characters that remind him of people he does not like very much. The teacher thought Johnny would be more creative and more accepting of the theme of the project if he associated the people he disliked with the fictional persons who would be murdered. She rationalized that this would help Johnny to proceed in this project with more attention to detail.

This is another example of moral relativism. If students are provided messages at school to seek out those things that make them feel good, they will increasingly cause more hurt for the people in their relationships. If students are allowed to express themselves in creative ways that endorse negative themes from movies, music, and other perceived social customs, they may feel that their views are acceptable. Johnny may have known that his teacher's intent was for him to be creative and was not to endorse murder. If Johnny was unable to differentiate this due to his irrational thinking caused by factors in his home and within himself, he could be susceptible to the influences of negative themes and discover maladaptive ways to resolve his problems with another person. What follows are real depictions of irrational thinking resulting in the most horrific kinds of hurt. These examples also present how a Johnny could turn to violence if he is not grounded in an absolute morality.

On May 21, 1998, fifteen-year-old Kipland Kinkel went to Thuston High School in Springfield, Oregon, and open fired in the cafeteria, killing two students and wounding twenty-two others. The night before, Kipland had killed his parents and spent the night with their dead bodies. He set up bombs in the house that were booby-trapped to go off prior to going to school, with the intention of killing as many people as possible. It was alleged that Kipland gave a talk in speech class about how he was going to create a bomb and torture animals. In a literature class, Kipland stood in front of his class and read from his journal and indicated he "planned to kill everyone."

On April 20, 1999, eighteen-year-old Eric Harris and seventeen-year-old Dylan Klebold opened fire in Columbine High

School, leaving twelve students and a teacher dead. Both boys died after suffering self-inflicted gunshot wounds. A diary found by police indicated that the two boys had been planning this massacre for over a year. The diary indicated that what triggered execution of the plan was when four popular athletes and another student from Columbine High School were arrested for felony burglary charges but were later left go with just a "slap on their wrist." It is alleged that this preferential treatment might have led to the massacre. The two boys made a video for a class in which they depicted a scene from the movie, "The Basketball Diaries." In the video, they portrayed themselves in trench coats going down a school hallway shooting at the jocks of the school. They portrayed the gunmen as their friends portrayed the jocks.

Public schools do not utilize a system that helps students to define and evaluate acceptable behavior, so students do not have a way of developing and evaluating good and bad behavior. They are made aware only when they break rules. Having rules without outlining positive behavioral expectations reinforces only those students who do not follow rules.

Whose Job Is It Anyway?

Whose job is it to teach children what constitutes good and bad behavior? Do you think the school has a responsibility to teach students morality? Schools take a neutral stance regarding morally charged issues. When a teacher entertains a student's right to express hurtful messages without challenging these negative views, he or she is indirectly endorsing violence.

In earlier decades, bullying, physical attacks, and theft would have constituted the majority of the negative behaviors observed in a school setting. Today this factor in the school setting contributes to the irrational thoughts of the students who are victimized. Have you ever been picked on in school? When students are on the receiving end of these hurtful behaviors, they sometimes go through extensive worry and anxiety-factors that impact learning and rational thought processes.

The National Center for Education Statistics (NCES) presented in 1993 that more elementary school children (29 percent) worried about being victims at school than high school students (20 percent). The NCES also reported that 73 percent of students in assigned public schools and 71 percent in public schools of choice reported having knowledge that either bullying, physical attacks, or robbery was occurring in the school compared to 45 percent of private school students in 1993. Twelve percent of the students in assigned public school, versus 7 percent in private schools, stated that they have personally experienced crime or threats in their school. Thirty-four percent of middle or junior high students were being victimized in school, as opposed to 20 percent of high school students. The statistics showed that 12% of middle or junior high students reported being bullied at school, which was twice the rate of high school students. Students entering high school have the lowest rates of bullying behavior (6 percent), and worry less about being bullied (20 percent) than elementary and middle school students. Eight percent of students in high school said they have been personally victimized.

There are additional surveys that demonstrate how bullying and harassing behavior has continued to exist in public school at a significant rate since the NCES report in 1993. In the March 2002 Educational Resources Information Center (ERIC) Digest 155, entitled, "Preventing Bullying," Ms. Linda Lumsden wrote that 30 percent of students in public schools in sixth through tenth grades reported to bully others, to be the target of bullies, or to experienced both. This data was collected from 15,000 sixth through tenth grade students across the United States. Ms. Lumsden also reported that a majority of the thirty-seven school shootings analyzed by the United States Secret Service classified shooters as victims of "bullying and harassment."

According to a 2001 Hostile Hallways survey of 2064 public school students in eighth through eleventh grades, Harris Interactive, a worldwide market research, polling, and consulting firm, reported how four out of every five students, boys and girls, claim to be sexually harassed in school. One out of four of the students reporting sexual harassment stated that the harassment occurred often. This report separated the sexual harassment into two categories; physical and non-physical. The physical sexual harassment included the unwanted removal of clothing in sexual ways and the forcing of sexual acts other than kissing. The non-physical sexual harassment included acts of taunting, spreading rumors, creating graffiti, telling jokes and making gestures. Approximately 76 percent of the students reported non-physical sexual harassment while 58 percent reported physical harassment. The report defined sexual harassment as unwanted and unwelcome sexual behavior that interferes with a person's life.

In a public school's system of discipline, faculty carry out punitive measures when students do not follow rules and guidelines. Detentions, suspensions, and expulsions are the main disciplinary measures in this system. There are occasions when a student needs to be protected from another student, especially in extremely volatile situations. In these cases, a student may need to be expelled from the school. Students are not taught coping and problem-solving skills in this type of system. The victim's anger and frustration can accumulate due to his or her irrational views concerning the problem, which thereby increases the threat of violent acts. The punitive measures do not provide a rational means of resolving conflict and hurt.

On March 1, 2001, fifteen-year-old Andy Williams opened fire on his school, killing two other students while wounding eleven other students and two teachers at the Santana High School in Santee, California. He allegedly told friends he wanted to "pull a Columbine," and no one took him seriously. Students at the school described Andy as "scrawny and little" and someone who "always got picked on." Andy stated that he made up his mind to carry out the attack three days before the incident. He said that he became disappointed and angry with the school for disciplining him for repeated tardiness.

On December 1, 1997, fourteen-year-old Michael Carneal killed three students and wounded five others at the Heath High School in Paducah, Kentucky. He shot eleven rounds of fire at a morning prayer circle in the lobby of the school. Mike was talked into surrendering his gun by one of the other students and told the principal he was sorry. Friends of Mike reported that he was emotionally immature and was picked on by some of the football players on occasion. They said, "He got it bad from some of the kids, but not as bad as some other kids get it around here." The principal of the school noted that essays and short stories revealed that Mike was constantly teased and picked on.

School suspensions or expulsions will not stop a relationship from becoming violent. When a student is placed in detention or is suspended, he is usually not asked to engage in any type of problem resolution activity. The student does not evaluate his behavior, develop ways to resolve the problem, and make amends to the hurt party. The victim fears retaliation due to the lack of closure regarding the hurtful act. Neither student is taught appropriate ways to manage anger and frustration. Any actions by either student would be a result of his irrational thought processes brought about by these strong feelings.

DEVELOPING BEHAVIORAL EXPECTATIONS IN THE SCHOOL ENVIRONMENT

Family and school settings need to develop systems that define behavioral expectations and allow children to evaluate their successes and problems. This system needs to include a way for problem solving to occur. This will help children to learn how to recognize their hurt and repair the hurt in a relationship. Don't you think that you would have benefited from this type of system? This will help children remain grounded in the rational mind-set that people who hurt others are accountable, and the relationship can be repaired through a problem resolution approach. The next two chapters will outline the categories from which these behavior expectations will be developed, along with strategies on selecting behaviors to improve a relationship. Individuals with psychiatric and developmental disabilities will also benefit from the same type of system.

The family or individual who wants to incorporate the behavioral expectations and problem-solving strategies outlined in the following chapters would need only to ensure that time is set aside each day to evaluate the positive or negative behaviors of all participants. This would also include time for problem solving to take place. In a school setting, additional factors will need to be considered when implementing this type of system. These factors will be discussed in the remainder of this chapter.

FACTOR 1: IDENTIFYING LEARNING DIFFERENCES

One factor that needs to be considered when this system is implemented in a school is the differences in how students learn based upon their developmental stage. Do you remember how you learned in the first years of school? Teachers will teach behavioral expectations and problem solving to children in early elementary school through indirect methods. This will include the use of stories and play activities to demonstrate each behavioral expectation. Once students reach the fourth grade, their teachers will utilize discussion times to teach expectations and to help students solve problems. As students enter middle and high school, the teacher will teach behavioral expectations and problem solving through role-plays and open group discussions initiated by the students. Students will need to test their views on morality and gain a sense of their identity and autonomy as they enter adolescence.

FACTOR 2: TEACHER AND STUDENT PARTICIPATION

The second factor that a school will need to consider while implementing this system is the level of participation by the teacher as compared to the student (again based upon the developmental stage of the student). Early elementary students will be less active in the development and evaluation of the behavioral expectations. The teacher will initiate most of the stories or play activities, depicting the behavioral expectations and prompting children to demonstrate them when relevant. The teacher will help students to evaluate how they met specific behavioral expectations and help them to identify and resolve problems. When students reach the fourth and fifth grades, the teacher will remain active in the development of behavioral expectations, but the students will be given more opportunities to evaluate whether they met the behavioral expectations. They will be provided opportunities to resolve conflicts with some guidance. In the middle and high schools, teachers will take a less active role in the development and evaluation of behavioral expectations. The teacher will ask the students to negotiate behavioral expectations based upon criteria presented in role-plays and open discussions. Students will choose expectations that will promote their meeting developmental needs.

FACTOR 3: MEANS OF EVALUATION

The third factor the school will need to consider while implementing this type of system is the means by which the students will evaluate their behavior and resolve issues when they fall short of the mark. For each group of students, teachers will utilize class and free periods to evaluate student behavior and conduct problem-solving activities. The elementary school students will have more opportunities to evaluate their behavior due to the smaller classroom sizes and fewer transitions to other classrooms during the school day. Teachers could use the beginning portion of a class to review behavioral expectations relevant to the activity, and then use the end of the class to review how students performed. Students could engage in problem-solving activities as problems occur.

EXAMPLE 1

Boy 1: I can't believe you broke my toy. I think you are a stupid idiot, and I hope you die.

Boy 2: I did not do it on purpose, and I think you are stupid. You are a freak and no one in class likes you.

Boy 1: We will see who the freak is when I punch you in the mouth.

Boy 2: Bring it on!

EXAMPLE 2: THE TEACHER MEDIATES

Boy 1: I can't believe you broke my toy. I think you are a stupid idiot and I hope you die.

Teacher: Boy 1, I can sense you are mad, so why don't we all sit down away from the other students who are doing their art work. Let's play this out with our toy characters. Boy 1, grab the superhero doll and talk to Boy 2's character about what he did to make you angry.

Boy 1: You made me feel mad when you broke my toy.

Teacher: Boy 2, use your doll to tell the superhero what happened and how breaking the toy made you feel.

Boy 2: I was riding your big wheel in the room too fast and hit into the teacher's desk. I did scratch the paint and feel bad that I hurt your big wheel.

Boy 1: That's OK, you did not do this on purpose.

Teacher: What can you do to make it up to the superhero?

Boy 2: I can let him use one of my toys for a whole day.

Teacher: How does that sound, Boy 1?

Boy 1: Sounds great!

Not every problem resolution activity will go smoothly or end with students taking responsibility for their hurtful behavior. The teacher will need to be patient and persevere through this process. Once each student becomes accustomed to the new problem-resolution norms and is reinforced for his positive participation, the problem-solving process will become easier. The teacher will be the key in determining the success or failure of the program.

TRANSITION TIMES AND STUDY HALLS

In middle and high school, teachers will experience more difficulties performing these same tasks with the increase in class sizes, the number of classes, and transition periods. Many students demonstrate behavioral problems during transition times. This is when threats, teasing, theft, and other acts of bullying occur. When behavioral expectations are not followed in the classroom, many teachers do not have the class time to allow students to evaluate their behavior.

Volunteers and school counselors can be used to monitor students during transition times and to mediate problem-solving activities as problems occur. Each teacher, counselor, and volunteer would have a list of the behavioral expectations for each group of students. In the present school system, students who demonstrate aggressive behavior are forced to wait for punitive actions to be taken by the principal. The hall monitors will work collaboratively with the school counselors and teachers to bring students together to resolve disputes as they occur throughout the school day. When a student refuses to solve a problem through the mediation of the hall monitor, he will be brought together with the principal and his parents to discuss the rationale behind his refusal. Many times, school personnel will get a better picture of a student's irrational thought processes after meeting with his or her parents. If the parents send negative messages to the student, the school administrator will gain more insight into the student's irrational thinking. Resistant students will need encouragement and support from their teachers, counselors, and other school personnel during their initial resistance.

Study halls and after-school times will need to be the times when groups of students meet to evaluate how each student met or did not meet the behavioral expectations. Teachers, school counselors, and volunteers will need experience or training in facilitating groups. The facilitators will need to create an environment in which responsibility, not perfection, is the expectation. The facilitator will need to perform a self-assessment of how he manages his own conflict and anger, so that he can safeguard against modeling codependent or aggressive traits.

Study halls will be a time when the groups are held, with each group consisting of six to eight students. Many schools may not have had the personnel to cover the amount of groups necessary to promote this program. Your school administrators would have needed to form collaborations with local human service agencies and county offices in order to access professionals who could provide school-based activities such as this group process. These professionals, along with volunteers and school counselors, may meet the needs of the students.

Group Therapy

Have you ever been part of a therapeutic group? Group therapy is a good forum in which to teach behavioral expectations and problem solving in the middle and high schools. This is where relationship skills can be generalized. With a trained facilitator who works to develop a cohesive group, students will be drawn to openly discuss their trials and tribulations with one another. The facilitator will create a forum in which to teach students and have them practice new skills in relevant ways.

The group will keep each of its members accountable to follow through with problem-solving activities. Group members will provide peer pressure to those who refuse to resolve conflicts. This will have a greater impact on resistant students than their receiving pressure from a group facilitator. As a teenager, did your peers influence you more than an adult? Each group will contain those students who will initially test the patience of the remaining members. Facilitators will need to allow for some distractions and for peer pressure to address the negative behavior.

Groups should consist of a gender and racial mix, if at all possible to allow students to test one another's beliefs and attitudes and to promote healthy conflict. This will promote realistic situations for students and prepare them for the adult world.

Since many of the behavioral expectations may not be demonstrated or evaluated in the classrooms, the group process will serve as a forum for students to practice and evaluate these behavior expectations. The group process will also serve as the forum in which students can practice problem solving through role-plays. Have you ever play-acted? Try it sometime. You will see how much fun this can be. The goal of the group would be to help students recognize their actions, both positive and negative, and resolve issues. This will be a system that is grounded in a rational approach to relationships.

The group process will teach students how to be assertive when communicating to students who hurt them. The facilitator's ability to prompt frustrated students to use "I statements" during escalating moments in the group is extremely important. The student's irrational instincts will be to verbally attack the other student or to withdraw. The facilitator will need to intervene and prompt students to take ownership for their thoughts and feelings. Have you ever been asked to make an "I statement"? This type of statement takes on the following structure: I (felt, thought, behaved) in such a manner because you acted in such a manner (in which I saw, heard, tasted, smelled, or touched).

John is a facilitator of an eight-member group at the local high school. His group consists of seniors, four female and four male students. The group has members who are athletes, honor students, work-study students, quiet students, and students who are considered "different" because of the way they dress and the way they express themselves. John has spent the first two weeks developing the rules of the group and discussing the need for each group participant to address the other participants by using "I statements" to indicate how others are impacting them. John says that participants have the right not to discuss those issues that are personal in nature and talks about the need for boundaries to be established. John reviews the need for the group members to share about those situations that they face in school this day during their interactions with students, teachers, and other school personnel. John also says that if students have personal issues to disclose, they need to see him after the session, and he will explain how to proceed.

John then discusses the rules of confidentiality: students who disclose issues regarding abuse or threats of harm to others or themselves will be breaking this rule. He would be responsible for disclosing this to protective services such as Children & Youth Services, the school-based counselor, or the local police. John reviews the tracking sheets that will be used as the starting points for each group. John goes over the behavioral expectations and has the group participants review and rehearse each of them. He then instructs the group that a review and rehearsal of these expectations will occur during the initial month as the group learns the rules and the process of the group.

The group will begin by having students summarize the previous group's themes and discussion points. This will ensure that the review of behavioral expectations and problem-solving activities was understood by all participants. John passes out the tracking forms to each participant and reviews how the tracking forms will serve as a starting point for today's group discussion. The session may then go as follows:

John: Can anyone summarize what the group discussed last session?

Bert (the athlete): We talked to Judy about how her acting stuck-up was disrespectful to others and how she needed to treat people better.

June (honor student): Bert, you know that you are not supposed to personally attack a group member like that! You are supposed to share how Judy's behavior affected you. I know I feel bad when Judy refuses to acknowledge my presence when I see her in the hall and at lunchtime.

Bert: I don't give a crap if she ever says anything to me! She is so weird and out there! I have more than enough friends and do not care about someone like her.

John: Bert, you are pretty angry toward someone who means very little to you. Let Judy know that you are mad and let her know why.

Bert: OK. Judy, I am angry with you because you treat me like I am not around. Everyone else in the school loves me and thinks I am a great guy.

Judy (the "different" student): How does it feel to have someone not give a shit about you?

Bert: Go to hell, bitch!

John: Let's back up here and remember the group rule concerning respect to others and not attacking others personally. Judy, you were making a statement to Bert about having someone not care about him. Could you make this same statement in the form of an "I statement"?

Judy: I feel upset at you Bert because you do not have any clue how someone like me feels. You have friends and are accepted by others while I get made fun of by you and every other student in this school.

Justin (work-study student): Judy, why do you give a shit what other people think? The hell with them all if they will not accept you for who you are!

John: Justin, why don't you tell Judy who she is based upon the definition we have reviewed about respect.

Justin: Judy, you are the most creative girl in the school. I have seen your drawings. You are very talented and would do anything for someone in need.

Bert: Let me see one of your drawings.

Judy: Here is one I drew of you while you were playing football.

Bert: Wow, you are good at art. Can I have this?

Judy: I guess so.

John: Bert and Judy, you both made some strong statements toward one another. How do you guys see this?

Bert: I was disrespectful to you, Judy. I did not know where you were coming from.

Judy: Me, too.

John: What can help you two get to know each other better? What could help you both gain better respect for one another?

Judy: Bert, we are in the same study hall each day. Do you want to hang out together?

Bert: Only if you can show me more drawings and allow me to show you some of my artwork without laughing.

Judy: That's a deal!

John: Good work, you two. Keep the group posted on how this is going between the two of you. Now, I want the group to get out their tracking sheets so we can go over how each of you have shown the qualities of love, respect, and honesty. I want to hear from some of the group members who have not said anything up to this point.

FACTOR 4: KEEPING TRACK

The fourth and final factor that the school will need to consider in order to implement this program is how to keep track of each student's actions, including his problem-resolution activities. A tracking sheet will be needed for each student in the school. This sheet will require teachers to identify each behavior that a student performs that meets a behavioral expectation. These behavioral expectations should not consist of behaviors in which students follow rules, or other activities that do not prompt the students to act. In the fourth chapter, behavioral expectations will be outlined for each developmental stage. This will serve as a guide for the types of behaviors that can be tracked by teachers.

In middle and high schools, tracking sheets will serve as a guide to help the group facilitator identify and reinforce positive behavior, since many teachers will not have time to evaluate student performance. Teachers can record how each student met certain expectations or identify when conflicts occurred. Since many conflicts occur during transition times, the problem-solving activities will occur outside of the group through the mediation of teachers, counselors, or hall monitors. Those conflicts that occur within a classroom setting will be "red flagged" by teachers on the tracking sheet and forwarded to the students' group facilitators. If students are working in separate groups, the group facilitators will determine what group will provide the best forum in which the students involved in the conflict can resolve the problem. If both students are from the same group, they would resolve their conflict within their own group setting.

The barriers to the success of this program will need to be addressed by school counselors, teachers, mediators, and administrative personnel on an ongoing basis. Regular staff meetings and supervision of all the personnel implementing the program will need to occur in order for the program to meet the students' needs. The school may need to utilize after-school hours for problem-solving activities.

The public school system is under pressure to demonstrate positive outcomes through standardized testing and to focus on the educational needs of students. Students are forced to cope with stress in a school environment that impacts their ability to achieve. The school administrators' decision to implement this system may lead to higher test scores of students due to their improved sense of security. Did you feel secure in your school settings? The growing concern of student and teacher safety in public schools needs to be addressed by school administrators.

Children need to develop a strong sense of right and wrong in order to be able to engage with others in positive ways. With a consistent message of appropriate versus inappropriate behavior, children will learn and demonstrate what is expected of them and respond positively to this structure. If a child has a psychiatric or developmental disability or is part of a family or school environment that de-emphasizes moral standards, he or she will view the world irrationally and not develop the social and emotional skills to form a healthy relationship. What are the moral standards that can bring you back to rational thinking after you have taken such an irrational ride through life? How can you work through developmental stages that you never attained? How will you recognize and repair hurt in your relationship? The next two chapters will provide you with answers to these questions.

Two

BEING MORAL MEANS YOU ALWAYS NEED TO SAY YOU'RE SORRY

The previous chapter introduced you to the terms *behavioral expectations* and *problem solving*. This chapter will place behavioral expectations into three categories in which an absolute morality will be based. There are many books and resources available that you can find that outline morals or virtues. Many of the virtues fall into three distinct categories. These consist of love, honesty, and respect. These virtues and their negative counterparts make up the foundation of human interactions.

Even when you make attempts to incorporate these virtues into your behavior, you will not always succeed. You will have instances when you will not love, respect, or show honesty with another person. Does this mean that you are bad or abusive? Your act of atoning is the key process that repairs the hurt that you inflict upon another person during these times. Atoning and problem solving are interchangeable. The sincerity of your atoning will be evaluated by how you can shift your actions to emulate the virtues of love, respect, and honesty. Making amends or reparations for a hurtful act is the best way to help you integrate the virtues of love, respect, and honesty. If you reflect back on those times when you have been on the receiving end of a sincere apology, you understand how powerful this process can be. Your hurt feelings were validated by the other person's willingness to accept responsibility for his or her behavior and to resolve the problem.

The concepts of virtues and morals will be used here frequently. As mentioned earlier, these terms are interchangeable and are considered good acts from an absolute standard. You may question by how this absolute standard is set. This standard is based upon definitions used for the virtues of honesty, love, and respect. Behavioral expectations can be developed from the definitions in each virtue category. The guiding principle to these absolutes is that an act that physically, sexually, or emotionally hurts someone is wrong. You may instantly claim you are a moral person based upon your initial thoughts. Physical and sexual hurt are easier to see than emotional hurt. You will need to read further to begin to rationally evaluate if whether you are hurting someone in subtle ways. You will need to understand each of the definitions of the three virtue categories.

You are cautioned not to evaluate your behavior based upon the antonym of each virtue. For example, you may claim that you were not dishonest, hateful, or disrespectful on any given day. The problem with looking at the opposite side of each virtue is that you are not promoting acts that demonstrate love, respect, and honesty. Using antonyms will allow for you to actually do nothing. This will be your initial instinct, since you will revert back to irrational thinking. You may want to avoid a change in your behavior and the conflict that may result within you.

Why is it important for you to have definitions outlined for each virtue? Many definitions that you have been taught about these virtues were based upon rules and codes of conduct. Rules and codes usually tell you what you should not do and not what you need to do. Some virtues were told to you as romantic tales involving feelings with no objective means to evaluate them. The definitions that follow are presented in an objective fashion to help you begin to develop behaviors that emulate each virtue.

Honesty is not only the act of telling the truth; it also involves ascertaining the truth about you. You most likely have never engaged in introspection and are oblivious to your negative patterns of interactions and the hurt that you are inflicting. In order for your relationship to improve, an honest evaluation must take place as to how you demonstrate love and respect. You may believe you are being truthful about your behavior. To test your thinking, you will need to learn the definitions of love and respect. If you cannot show how you have demonstrated each of those virtues, you have not honestly evaluated your behavior.

Love is a virtue that can be demonstrated in a multitude of ways. Many of the definitions found in Webster's New World Dictionary relate love to a feeling ñ —"a passionate affection of one person for another." I will add two elements to the definition of love: love requires action, and love is unconditional. Love involves acts of kindness or generosity that do not require response. Showing love involves displaying feelings, but feelings should not be the driving force in how or why you demonstrate love. If you reserve your love only for those who make you feel good, you would will tend to withhold love more often. Children can sometimes display behavior that arouses feelings in parents that may not be loving. During those times, feelings of anger and frustration can cause parents to put their children down and to place conditions on their love for them.

Respect entails the ability to appreciate and bring out the unique qualities of others while placing value on their opinions and abilities. Many times, each person in a relationship may emphasize the negative attributes of the other. Those who are negatively impacted may begin to shift their focus from developing special talents to repairing physical or character flaws. Have you or the person in your relationship thought about getting cosmetic surgery, experienced dissatisfaction at work, or experienced stagnation? The absence of respect may make it difficult for either one of you to appreciate and develop natural gifts and talents.

What makes these virtues based on absolutes different from the morals based on social customs? Doesn't society place value on the concepts of respect, honesty, and love? While reading the previous chapter, you were introduced to some of the social customs of families and schools. The concepts of honesty, love, and respect are not found in your daily paper, the classroom setting, family discussions, or in many of your community activities. Is this a topic that you discuss with friends, family, or coworkers? What do you talk about? Many people focus their discussions on what they fear, want, envy, or feel deprived of. They focus their energies on finding those things that will make them feel good and hurt others along the way. This is how moral relativism can influence a person's actions. This is not to suggest that people do not want to emulate good acts or do the right thing with persons in their relationships. They have either lost or not discovered a way to define good behavior or the right thing to do.

From the examples in this book, you should have a clearer picture of how relativistic views on morality contribute to irrational thinking. Is it rational to pursue pleasure all the time? Can you justify hurting someone because things are not going your way? Should you have sex with whomever, whenever you please?

These questions will be easier to answer when you evaluate each question based on the virtues of honesty, respect, and love. You would be hard pressed to prove that you can spend most of your time seeking pleasurable experiences while maintaining respect, honesty, and love in your relationship. The same could be said for rationalizing hurt and engaging in sex outside your relationship. Following absolute standards is what will ground your relationship in the truth. The truth will come from rational thoughts, resulting from your emulating concrete virtues.

Responsibility and *accountability* should not be scary words to you. You should be comfortable with these terms that are part of knowing when you are doing the right or wrong thing. When you begin to understand these virtues better and incorporate them into your daily living, you will invite the opportunity to take ownership for your good and bad behavior. You will accept your human nature to make mistakes and will want to repair the hurt through an atoning act.

You should not try to ignore the impact of the hurt you have caused, because you will become a better person from your struggle to discern what is right and wrong. Imperfections are what make your life challenging and rewarding. You can work through humiliation, conflict, and other difficulties in your relationship to gain valuable life skills. The fight to do the right thing will become the foundation of your growth as an individual. In order to grow, you must learn how to display responsibility, accountability, and acts of reconciliation for those times when you do not do the right thing. Undoubtedly, you will hurt others even when you have their best interests in mind. Through atonement or problem resolution, you can take responsibility for hurtful actions and demonstrate acts of love, respect, and honesty. If your acts of hurt, both subtle and violent, continue to occur without your taking responsibility, your partner in your relationship will grow distant from you. He or she may end all contact. Do you really want this to happen? You may end up doing something you will regret the rest of your life.

Jane and her husband were very happy together. Jack had always had a short fuse when under stress. Jane knew Jack always had her best interests in mind. Jack was a hard worker and worked several jobs to keep the family living in their four-bedroom home. The couple was so proud of their two girls. They were so beautiful. Jack was under a lot of stress at his jobs and had not been sleeping well. He fell into more verbal outbursts and made statements about wishing the stress of family and work could all be over. Jane had just started a part-time job to help alleviate some of the financial burden, which allowed Jack to quit one of his jobs. Maggie was the youngest daughter, only a year old. She cried a lot and experienced difficulties sleeping. Jack was watching the girls one night and could not get Maggie to quiet down and fall asleep. Jack had always exercised great patience with Maggie. On this night, Jack picked Maggie up and shook her, pleading with her to keep quiet. Maggie died from the trauma caused by Jack's actions.

You have a responsibility to understand how stress and your past impact your behavior in respect to how you treat others. You cannot go through life not recognizing the hurt that you cause. If you do, you will hurt people just as you have been hurt in your past. The stress of life is only going to increase as life moves at faster and faster speeds. If you want to know how fast life is moving, check with your Internet provider!

How many times have you said you are doing the best you can do? How many times have you said this after you have hurt someone? Hurting another person is not the best that you or anyone else can do. If you want to guard yourself from crossing the line between subtle hurt and acts of violence, you should consider assessing your behavior on a daily basis. As you commit to a system that helps you to develop behavioral expectations for the virtues of love, respect, and honesty, you will begin to recognize and repair the hurt in your relationship. The next chapter will show you how to develop behavioral expectations and atoning strategies for each of the developmental stages of your life based on this absolute morality.

THREE

VIRTUES AND ATONEMENT

You have been introduced to the concept of an absolute morality. The virtues of love, respect, and honesty are the three categories that make the distinction between good and bad behavior. In the first three chapters, you have learned about factors that have contributed to your irrational thinking. You have also learned how your irrational thoughts can lead to your acts of hurt toward another person. Your developmental stages may have been impacted by these factors and caused you to develop more slowly than others, which further contributes to your relationship problems. In order to implement the virtues and the atonement process in your relationship, you will need to look back and examine each of the developmental stages that you have not met. You may not remember if you met the milestones of the stages of your childhood development. Perhaps you are just starting to develop some new insights and may still have difficulty recognizing what skills you need to develop. To be sure that you are working toward repairing your relationship, you may want to use some of the behavioral expectations from each developmental stage.

Begin with the earliest developmental stage in which you have not met the behavioral expectations of love, respect, and honesty. With the help of the other person in your relationship, make a list of all the behaviors you need to evaluate. Practice these behaviors, and evaluate yourself regularly. Once you demonstrate these behaviors consistently, you can go to the next developmental stage and include these new expectations as part of your daily evaluation. Your list of behaviors will be cumulative as you master developmental stages and enter new ones. This chapter will outline behavioral expectations for each developmental stage, under the virtue categories of love, respect, and honesty. Atoning behavior will also be presented in each developmental stage.

The descriptions of the milestones that need to be met in each developmental stage come from Erikson's Developmental Theory, taken from the book, *I Never Knew I Had a Choice,* by Gerald and Marianne Schneider Corey. No matter what your age or developmental stage, you will be able to refer to these behavioral expectations when you implement a virtue/atonement system in the relationships you encounter. The initial developmental stage will be described first, but it is the only stage that will not be practiced in the order discussed. Since this stage involves the development of trust, you will need to work through the other stages—thereby gaining a better understanding of the virtues of love, respect, and honesty—before you can establish whether you are in a trusting relationship. You will have a better opportunity to know the criteria on which you can base your trust of another person after you work through the rest of the stages of development.

STAGE 1: TRUST

When you were born, you possessed a developmental need for trust in your relationship with a parent or caretaker. You relied solely on a parent to care for your physical, social, and emotional needs. Although you do not remember your first year of life, you will know by the time you reach adulthood if you experience difficulties trusting others. Are you suspicious of the person in your relationship? On what do you base your suspicions? Have you trusted someone who later took advantage of your confidence? Many persons who have been physically, sexually, or emotionally abused as children lose their ability to determine whom they can trust. This can also be said for persons who suffer from serious mental and developmental disabilities. Although these people may have gone through their first year of life receiving the nurturing necessary to meet this milestone, a disability or the trauma of abuse and neglect later in their lives delayed their development.

BOUNDARIES

Before you can develop behavioral expectations in this stage, you will need to learn the concept of personal boundaries. Boundaries can be defined as borders or limits that can be imposed in physical, sexual, or emotional forms. If a person has been hurt traumatically or repeatedly over time, he would have experienced a violation of these boundaries. This can contribute to his inability to trust another person. A person with a mental or developmental disability would also experience problems understanding the concept of boundaries. As mentioned earlier, disabilities and trauma are factors that contribute to a person's irrational thinking. In turn, he may have trouble differentiating among the various types of relationships. He might see everyone as untrustworthy, or he may view them as trustworthy without any rational basis for this determination. In this stage of development, you will initially determine a person's trustworthiness based on his or her ability to demonstrate love, respect, and honesty toward you. After determining that the person can be trusted, you will then allow a nurturing relationship to develop. Do you allow the person with whom you are involved in an intimate relationship to take care of your emotional and physical needs? Can you become vulnerable to someone once you have determined that you can trust him? Do you have to be in control at all times? Many people who have been hurt as children grow up with the irrational thought either that they must be in control at all times or that they cannot control anything in their lives.

Boundaries can be established with another person by changing the frequency of contact, the content of the disclosures during contact, and the physical and sexual distances created. Without boundaries, a person can lose the ability to protect himself in physical, sexual, and emotional ways. Relationships can fall under several categories: intimate, friend, acquaintance, or stranger. Intimate relationships can include friends. Intimates are those persons with whom you frequently have contact, disclose personal information during contacts, and experience close physical, emotional, or sexual contact. These relationships take much work to maintain and should be with people with whom you want to spend the majority of your time. Remember, however, that physical and emotional closeness is not to be confused with sexuality. You can have intimate friends whom you allow to come close to you in physical yet non-sexual ways.

Acquaintances are persons whom you have seen before but with whom you choose not to pursue contact, other than running into them in community places or at work. This type of relationship can consist of people you see often but have not chosen to share any extra time with or to disclose any information other than current events, publicly known information, or work-related information. Strangers are those people not known to you. In relationships with acquaintances or strangers, the frequency of contact, the type of disclosure, and the degree of physical, emotional, and sexual closeness have an impact. You would maintain a personal boundary with acquaintances and strangers by minimizing your personal contact, refraining from making personal disclosures, and not becoming physically, sexually, or emotionally involved with them.

As you develop behavioral expectations in the three virtue categories, you may discover that you have intimate relationships from which you need to distance yourself because those people are continually hurting you and yet not atoning for that hurt. In this stage of development, it is important to put your trust in an absolute standard. Once you understand how the virtues operate in each developmental stage, you will be better equipped to assess whether trust can be established in your relationship.

What can you do to allow trust to develop in your relationship? You have determined that this person is someone with whom you want to be close and share intimacy. How can you make yourself more vulnerable to this person? A person can experience hurt in a relationship when the other person does not expose his or her vulnerable side. The way to become vulnerable is to share your insecurities, fears, hopes, dreams, and your need for the other person. By practicing the virtues in this stage, you can come to accept the other person in his own demonstrations of love, respect, and honesty toward you. A good idea is to ask the other person to share his thoughts and feelings about your actions.

LOVE

As you are developing trust, one way in which you can practice love is by allowing the other person to come in close physical contact with you and by enjoying the feeling of closeness. Do you let the other person in your relationship hold you without questioning his or her act of love? This is a time to be nurtured, not a time to look for ulterior motives in that person's act of love. Perhaps you instinctively want to pull away or to focus your time on other, more distracting activities. But this will only serve to contribute to your irrational thoughts, and you will not be showing your love for the other person. You will need to allow the other person to perform other acts of kindness, such as massaging the body, making favorite meals, and writing letters of love. Have you discussed a favorite activity or interest of yours and allowed the other person in your relationship to be part of the experience with you? By allowing the other person into your world, you are not only developing trust, but also earning trust.

RESPECT

How can you show respect in this developmental stage, while you are developing trust? You should make time each day to share a fear, dream, or hope, and to let the other person in your relationship know how he or she can share in this experience. By including the other person in these thoughts and feelings, you will enhance the relationship. Respect entails a concerted effort, each person taking time to value the other. Do you accept compliments from the other person in your relationship? Most people who do not trust others will not accept a compliment without minimizing the statement in some manner. They do not thank the person for making the compliment because they do not believe the statement.

HONESTY

Under the category of honesty, you can evaluate your ability to trust by participating in daily conversations with the other person about how well you are demonstrating love and respect. This discussion will also include how well you have shared your vulnerabilities. People who are developing trust need to let others know how comfortable or uncomfortable they are with the expectations involved in showing love and respect. Through honest communication and the use of "I statements," you can work to reach a compromise on how fast the behavioral expectations are incorporated. Both parties in a relationship that is building trust need to keep the other's vulnerabilities confidential. Violating the other's confidence will hurt the trust that both are attempting to establish.

For those areas in which you fall short of the mark, thereby hurting another, you will need to take responsibility for your actions and atone for the hurt you have caused. Sometimes people who do not live up to certain behavioral expectations do not initially recognize the impact of the hurt they cause. For instance, even though you committed a hurtful act, you may feel as though you were being helpful by not requiring love and respect from the other person. However, the system of responsibility and atonement is intended to help both persons in a relationship to demonstrate these virtues. Once you take responsibility for your hurtful action, you can atone for it by beginning to demonstrate the behavior you were previously unable to perform. If through discussions and problem solving you both discover that the expectation in question is not attainable at the time, you can make amends by sharing your sorrow and your appreciation for the other person's attempts to show love, respect, or honesty. You can also communicate the steps that you will take to meet this expectation in the future.

Over time, as you are developing trust, you will need to

reciprocate the acts of love and respect as outlined in this developmental stage. You should not wait too long to do this. Selfless acts are what will help you to understand the powerful impact this system can have in each relationship you encounter.

STAGE 2: AUTONOMY VS. SELF-DOUBT

In the next stage of development (ages 1–3), the core struggle is autonomy versus shame and self-doubt. A person's ability to express his individuality is very important in this stage. Making mistakes, challenging the status quo, and critical thinking are the ways in which a person is able to express his individuality. A person who is criticized and made to feel unworthy will not meet the milestones for this stage. Many people adapt to these negative messages by accepting the status quo and emulating the qualities of the people who are significant to them. Even at a young age, many of these individuals develop codependent traits and perfectionist tendencies in order to survive in this type of environment.

The virtues that will be established for this developmental stage will focus on your individuality and dependency. Having genuine thoughts, feelings, and behaviors is important in this stage. You will need to be able to demonstrate appropriate ways of depending on the other person in your relationship. Many people experience difficulties exercising their individuality and dependency in healthy ways. In many relationships, one person gets hurt when the other asks either too much or too little from him. This stage does not include household responsibilities or other tasks. Rather, the focus is on solving problems and thinking in original ways. People who can make decisions based on the facts and a sense of right and wrong demonstrate critical thinking skills. On the other hand, people who avoid making a decision and rely on others to solve problems have not met this developmental stage. Additionally, people who do not include others in making decisions when the outcome affects both persons are not demonstrating a healthy dependency. What do you depend on from the other person in your relationship? Who makes the decisions in your relationship? Whom do your decisions impact?

Love

To demonstrate love in this stage, you must develop behavioral expectations that center on performing unconditional acts of charity that also demonstrate your individuality. How would you want to show the other person that you love him? Are your acts of love original or copied from scenes from a book or movie? Singing songs, writing letters, dancing, painting pictures, or simply wrapping oneself up as a present are a few of the thousands of ways in which a person can demonstrate love. You will need to erase the images of love that you have seen on commercials and soap operas. Then you will need to establish acts of unconditional love that are based on your own personal creativity. Let the other person in your relationship know how much that you depend on his or her love. When you demonstrate these original acts of love to one another, both of you should specifically explain what you find enjoyable about them. This is how behavioral expectations in this area can be renegotiated over time.

Respect

To demonstrate the virtue of respect, it is important to recognize the attributes of the other person in your relationship and allow him to make mistakes. If you have unmet needs in this developmental stage, you will most likely develop perfectionist characteristics. This being the case, you would have the tendency to notice the mistakes of the other person while not acknowledging his positive qualities. In order to correct this, you will need to develop a list of behavioral expectations that demonstrate your ability to recognize the accomplishments of the other person. This may be difficult to do when you first get started because it will force you to shift from irrational to rational thinking. When you recognize someone doing something well, you are acting in a positive and rational way. This does not mean that you should ignore behavior that is disrespectful to you. You may discover that many of the mistakes the other person makes have little or no impact on you. In these cases, you could demonstrate respect by not recognizing the mistakes and by recognizing the accomplishments. You will find that the other person will usually reciprocate this act.

It may be a good idea to set a certain number of times each day when you will catch the other person performing well. This will allow the other person to further explore his individual talents and to utilize his critical thinking skills. Catching the other person making a mistake will only hurt his self-esteem.

Respect in this stage also involves valuing the opinion of others. When decisions need to be made that impact the two people in a relationship, you can let the other person know how much you value his opinion. Making purchases, saving money, disciplining children, making job changes, and other decisions impacting both parties are examples of decisions that could be made together.

You will also need to demonstrate your unique talents in solving problems that arise at work, at school, and in the community. Begin to address barriers in your life in these areas. Many people experience problems with work, school, or the community because they lack knowledge, organization, confidence, or motivation. In this stage of development, you will need to develop behavioral expectations that target ways of increasing learning and organization within your activities in these areas. Ask for clarification or help in order to increase your knowledge and to learn the culture of each environment. Evaluate how you acquired knowledge and organized your activities each day. The expectations will also include ways in which you made decisions in a rational way. You will need to practice how to make decisions in sequential steps by defining the problem, exploring options and personal preferences, and committing to a decision based on the consequences of each option. This will help to promote your individuality in these areas and less dependency on others.

HONESTY

In the area of honesty, you will need to evaluate how you demonstrated love and respect as it has been outlined here. You must be willing to take responsibility for those times when you did not attempt to show love or were critical of the other person in your relationship. Have you demonstrated too much dependency or individuality? During the daily evaluation of virtues, communicate your thoughts, and talk about stressful events with the other person. Take responsibility for those times when you were not demonstrating love and respect because of stressful events and irrational thoughts. At this point, you can atone for the hurt you've caused by making a plan to demonstrate love and respect in the area where you were unable to meet expectations.

STAGE 3: MORAL REASONING

The third developmental stage contains milestones that are characterized in a person's preschool years (ages 3–6). A person does not formulate the ability for moral reasoning until this stage. This is when a person acquires a sense of right and wrong. One of the milestones of this stage is to develop a sense of competence and initiative. Children learn to give and receive love at this stage. They learn how to jump, roll, throw, run, kick, and say their ABCs. Children whose choices are restricted or made for them will generally withdrawal due to their feelings of guilt and shame. As a child, did you have the ability to initiate activities that you enjoyed? Were you able to express your love to a parent? Did you develop the physical skills to participate in physical activities with other children? People who are unable to express love or initiate the activities they enjoy will tend to isolate themselves from others. They never learn the basic social, physical, and emotional skills needed to relate to other people. As adults, these people experience difficulties demonstrating love. They feel awkward in social situations and tend to engage only in those activities in which they have gained competency. Without a balanced approach to work, family, friends, recreation, and other leisure activities, these people do not gain the competencies needed to relate to another person in a relationship. Many times, these people will overcompensate for their insecurities by demanding that others recognize them for their area of competency.

LOVE

When you consider the three virtue categories of love, respect, and honesty, what sorts of behavioral expectations are involved with this stage? One way in which you can demonstrate love is to gain a balance in among your activities: work, family, friends, and recreation. You can demonstrate unconditional acts of love by participating in the activities of the other person in your relationship. This may mean that you will engage in activities in which you do not have a competency or comfort level. Through your participation, however, you can develop the social and physical skills needed to increase your comfort levels. You may want to test the irrational thought that you must have competency in an activity in order to participate. Of course, this is a rational thought for those activities in which incompetence may have lethal consequences.

You will also need to take time to perform loving acts not only for the other person in your relationship, but also for those outside of the relationship. Spending time with an elderly neighbor, teenager, or a child engaged in a fun activity will not only help you to develop your sense of love, but it will also allow you to continue developing you physical and social skills. Do you know of any child, teenager, or elderly person who enjoys recreational or leisure activities? When is the last time you threw a ball, rolled down a hill, played tag, went fishing, or climbed a tree?

RESPECT

From the behavioral expectations delineated under love, you can also develop behavioral expectations for respect. If you are engaged in an activity that involves someone else, you will want to show that you value the unique qualities of the other person. This will be difficult you if you have isolated yourself from others and have placed too much value on your own competence. However, it is important to recognize others and their need to feel competent and special. To enhance any relationship, compliments must be reciprocated, for they show sincere respect.

HONESTY

In the area of honesty, you will need to evaluate your efforts to demonstrate love and respect as outlined in the preceding paragraphs. Honestly assess your willingness to try new activities and to recognize the positive attributes in others. When you do not act in loving or respectful ways, do you take responsibility for the hurt that you caused? You can atone by carrying out a plan to meet with the person you hurt and by demonstrating an act of love or respect as outlined in your behavioral list. If you discover that a child, teenager, or other adult does not want to spend time with you, then take a moment to evaluate what took place during your interactions with that person. What were the topics of the discussions? Who initiated the discussion? What did you learn about the other person, and what did you reveal about yourself? You cannot expect a relationship to form when the conversation goes only one way. If you have dominated the discussion topics, the other person has not had the opportunity to demonstrate his or her knowledge and other unique talents.

STAGE 4: INDUSTRY VS. INFERIORITY

The next stage of development is the middle childhood years (ages 6–12). The key developmental tasks are to engage in social activities, to expand knowledge in many areas, to accept differences in people, to develop cooperative skills, and to further develop physical skills. The struggle that a person experiences in this stage is between industry and inferiority. A person would need to achieve goals while keeping a proper perspective on his or her failures. The expectations of the person's parents at this stage can influence his or her self-concept. Expectations that are too high or low will contribute to a person's irrational thoughts regarding his or her ability to meet or not meet goals. This is the stage when a person develops his or her morality.

What morals do you prescribe? What criteria do you use to determine whether you relate to someone in a good or bad way? Many children are influenced by their parents to adopt the same prejudices and morality. Others adopt the morality of external influences such as television and music. When a person does not adapt to differences, cooperate with others, or understand good and bad behavior, he will have unmet milestones in this developmental stage.

Love

The behavioral expectations you develop for the virtue of love will need to reflect acts of charity toward people who are different from you, whether in race, gender, ethnicity, or beliefs. Perhaps you can volunteer at a local charity; this will expose you to different cultures and beliefs, thereby helping you to expand your knowledge as well as adapt to new experiences. Working in a soup kitchen for the homeless, handing out food at a local food bank, or supporting a charitable cause for other ethnic groups are just some of the ways in which love can be demonstrated.

Respect

To demonstrate respect, you can ask another person to help you demonstrate cooperation. Start by exchanging ideas in a give-and-take fashion. Allow the other person to state his or her views during a conversation, and then give value to what is presented. This does not mean you have to agree with what is said. You will also need to show that you can take turns while engaged in a "sharing activity" with another person. Many adults have never learned to share or take turns. Do you share the remote control in your house? How do you arrange for tasks to be shared?

People can take turns making a meal, caring for a child, performing a chore, selecting activities, and other tasks that impact both individuals.

Honesty

To demonstrate honesty in this developmental stage, you will need to process the knowledge and experiences that you have gained through your acts of love and respect. Make an honest value judgement by comparing your preconceived notions with the reality of your experiences. As you evaluate your daily acts of love and respect, you will develop a better concept of your morality. You will see that the world is not simply black and white; rather, the diversity of others contributes to your understanding of the human condition. Through this understanding of diversity, you will begin to develop the insight that there are common themes of love and respect that bridge any difference. You will need to take responsibility for times when you have not demonstrated love and respect according to these expectations. Then, atone for that hurt by performing the behavioral expectation with the person you have hurt.

Stage 5: Emotional Maturity

The next developmental stage is adolescence (ages 12–18). The goal for individuals in this stage is to develop emotional maturity. Upon reaching this stage, you will need to find meaning in your life, as well as role models in whom you can believe. You need to gain a sense of individualism in order to establish your identity and to assume adult roles. If you lived with parents who either opposed your every move by narrowing your options or allowed too much freedom of choice, you would likely experience problems meeting the milestones in this stage.

Perhaps the biggest obstacle in your pursuit of individuality was a parent—a parent who was either too restrictive or to loose with you. This has resulted in some difficulties as you reached adulthood. The parent may have avoided confrontations with you and allowed you to explore your world without limits. Or, on the contrary, the parent may have been too confrontational and overprotected you from outside experiences. The parent–teenager relationship is often like a tug-of-war. If a parent pulls too hard, restricting the child's activities, the child pulls just as hard in the other direction. This is why a teenager will become rebellious: it is the only plan of action for this person when he is not afforded the opportunity to negotiate or work through problems with a parent. On the other hand, if a parent lets go of the rope and does not put any rules or guidelines in place, the teenager will fall due to the lack of guidance and accountability.

Parents need to learn how to pull the rope when their children begin to go beyond negotiated rules, and to loosen the rope when they demonstrate responsibility and trust. This can be done through a system that reinforces the virtues of love, respect, and honesty. With this system in place, a young person can explore options and roles, and he can further develop his morality.

As a teenager, did you know who you were, where you were going, and how you were going to get there? How would you answer this question today? Many people go through their lives without setting a course for themselves. They do not possess confidence and foresight because they lack adult-guided experiences that would help them to formulate their identity and virtues. Due to their lack of confidence, they become very insecure and susceptible to "quick fixes" in order to feel good and escape their fears and anxieties. To begin to develop individuality—and to define your identity and morality—you must create a path for your life based on the insights you've gained from new experiences. You will also need to use the virtues of love, respect, and honesty to guide you in these new experiences as you interact with others.

Love

To demonstrate love, you will need to create behavioral expectations based on your ability to perform adult roles in which you can demonstrate individuality. This will differ from the second stage of development (ages 1–3) in that this individuality is based on developing adult skills. These skills include performing the activities of daily living, and resolving problems and dilemmas. It is important in this stage to know that you can take care of yourself. If you can cook, clean, follow a budget, wash clothes, plan purchases, keep a job, structure time, and resolve problems, then you would demonstrate love to another person by sharing in these activities. This also helps you to gain more experiences and explore multiple roles in your relationship. You can demonstrate love by taking on new challenges that show your willingness to be responsible. However, you must not make demands on others while you take on these additional responsibilities. If conflicts arise in the process of taking on new responsibilities, you will need to demonstrate conflict resolution skills. You can also demonstrate love by giving your time or money to those you come in contact with. Helping a coworker, student, friend, or family member to resolve a problem, or providing monetary gifts, would also demonstrate love.

Respect

You can demonstrate respect by working through the dilemmas and conflicts that arise when taking on additional responsibilities. Negotiation is an important skill; during a conflict it shows that you have respect for the other person. You will need to develop problem-resolution skills that demonstrate personal responsibility. When conflict arises, address the problem by stating what you are planning to change about your behavior to resolve the issue. Through your ability to model accountability and ownership for problems, you will set the stage for positive communication and decision-making. You will also show that you value the other person by not projecting blame on him or her. Behavioral expectations in this stage include being able to identify your role in problem situations, accepting responsibility, and making positive changes in your behavior in order to resolve the issue.

One of the best ways to communicate your disagreement with another person's view is to use "I statements." This entails making statements that demonstrate your own responsibility for how you feel, think, and behave, while simultaneously presenting an objective observation of the actions that may have provoked those feelings, thoughts, or behaviors. To test the objectivity of a statement, you will need to show that the statement is based on what you saw, heard, tasted, smelled, or touched. This will help you to communicate in a way that demonstrates respect while also challenging views and beliefs that go against your own belief system. This is how you begin to test your own morality with others in the world.

"I statements" are an effective communication style during any conversation. This behavioral expectation will take practice and is a very important skill in any relationship. Because of the way an "I statement" is structured, you will not be able to blame the other person for how you feel, think, or behave. You will let the other person know what he or she did to provoke the feeling, thought, or behavior. "I hate you" does not communicate a message as effectively as, "I feel anger toward you because I heard you tell someone that I was stupid." Your ability to reach a compromised solution based on your discovery of a common belief with the other person is also necessary. When you continue to communicate in this fashion, you will soon discover that there are shared visions on what solutions will benefit each party. You will also demonstrate respect by asking for help when you lack enough understanding to resolve a particular problem.

Another way in which you can demonstrate respect is by valuing others through meaningful conversation. People in this stage need to develop interpersonal skills that allow them to identify with others in their peer group, as well with those they interact with in their other roles. In order to grow in this stage, you will need to develop skills by which you can introduce yourself to another person and enter into conversations that give value to others' views. Many adults never learn how to engage in a two-way conversation that communicates how much they value the other person. They either dominate the conversation, or they do not contribute enough to what is being discussed. Your ability to meet behavioral expectations in this stage will depend on your ability to make positive statements and to ask questions that demonstrate an interest in the other person's talents and abilities.

What do you communicate to others in the roles that you assume? Do you say anything to others to let them know that you value them? Do you know enough about the person to appreciate their talents and abilities? Your ability to introduce yourself to a new acquaintance is a behavioral expectation that demonstrates respect. Another expectation is your ability to find out about another person by asking open-ended questions. You will need to do more than ask, "How are you doing?" Asking questions that begin with what, where, when, how, and why can enhance the communication because they ask for more information than a one-word answer. This is not to say that you need to do this with every person you meet. Rather, if you want to pursue a relationship with a person, or if you are responsible for maintaining a positive relationship in a particular role, you will need to demonstrate these communication skills. How do you feel about a person who asks you about your talents and abilities?

HONESTY

The virtue of honesty is seen in a person's ability to take responsibility for his own thoughts, feelings, and behavior. In this developmental stage, you will need to evaluate whether or not your thoughts, feelings, and behavior were hurtful to another person. Your guide in making this determination will be the behavioral expectations developed in the areas of love and respect. You can engage in a variety of atoning acts in order to express your sorrow for those times when you did not meet the behavioral expectations. When you resolve problems through the behavioral expectations outlined above, you will be able to atone for the hurt you may have caused in a relationship.

Negotiating terms and following through with commitments will be important skills to develop in this stage. The following is an example of how an adolescent would demonstrate and evaluate the virtues discussed.

KEEPING COMMITMENTS

Rachel is a sixteen-year-old girl who wants to spend more

time with her friends. She wants to frequent the mall with her friends, go to parties, and drive her friends to restaurants, the movies, and other teenage hangouts. Rachel's parents have negotiated behavioral expectations in the areas of love, respect, and honesty. Rachel is asked to evaluate her behavior each day and atone for behavioral expectations she has not followed. The following is the dialogue between Rachel and her parents, and the atonement, which serves as the "tugging of the rope" when Rachel falls short of the expectations.

Mother: Rachel, you came in one hour past your curfew last night. This was a time we negotiated, and you agreed to follow it. What were you doing for the one hour when you were late?

Rachel: My friends and I were watching a great movie at Janie's house, and I did not want to be the only person who left. Your rules are too strict!

Father: You are blaming us for the curfew rule when you were part of the decision-making for this rule. Whose problem is this?

Rachel: Okay, it's mine, but I was only watching a movie at my girlfriend's house.

Mother: Why do you think we are really questioning this?

Rachel: You tell me. I do not see the big deal here.

Mother: Part of gaining trust so that you can do all the activities you want to do is following commitments that you make.

Father: So, what was the problem in this case?

Rachel: I did not follow the rules that I agreed to.

Father: What can you do to show us you can be trusted to follow through with commitments you make?

Rachel: I will be in early one hour each day for the next week.

Mother: That is a good way to show us that you are sorry and that you understand the importance of an honest relationship with us.

Father: Let's talk about the other expectations that you have met this day. You have really considered our views and have been complimentary of your mother's work.

One week later…

Rachel: I was able to be in one hour early each day this week. I enjoyed the time at home, got caught up on some extra-credit work for school, and was able to organize my bedroom.

Mother: I really appreciate your honesty and your being able to meet your commitments.

Father: Rachel, you have also showed many acts this past day that have really showed me you are respecting and loving others. Can you review these with us?

Rachel: I spent time with Mrs. Wilson today. She really enjoys when I read to her. I really see how her blindness has changed her priorities in the world. I was able to take some of my clothes to the Goodwill today. I had a hard time doing this cause I love my stuff. I got some help in school from someone that I have avoided. She is so smart, and I let her know how much I needed her help in physics. I also asked my boss for help at the restaurant. He was happy to spend time with me to show me how to use the cash register.

Mother: I know I was too hard on you today when you came home from school. I should not take out my anger on you when I get behind in my work. I will make sure that you and I go to one of your favorite places tomorrow.

Father: Since you have showed a willingness to stick to your commitments, your mother and I have decided to let you take the car to the movies with your friends. We will need to negotiate the terms of this new experience. Can you come up with any terms?

Rachel: I will drive to the movies and come straight home after the movie is over.

Mother: That sounds like responsible terms. If this works out, we will discuss other ways you can start to experience the other activities you have said you would like to do.

For many people, the act of problem-solving and reconciliation is difficult. From the time when they were very young, they have stayed away from people with whom they are in conflict. These people are taught to avoid tough situations that may provoke intense emotions because there will be opposing views. They are taught a type of learned helplessness, avoidance, and codependency. Many people in this developmental stage will want to be liked more than respected, so they will not share their honest views with others. Do you give in to peer pressure and the expectations of others when your morality is challenged?

Stage 6: Responsibility and Independence

Adulthood is a developmental stage that is marked by increased responsibility and independence. In this stage you will develop your ability to make your own decisions based on your personal morality. However, you must be able to discern how your parents and others either positively or negatively influenced your decision-making and virtues. In other words, you need to gain self-awareness and understand the truth about your upbringing. You will not achieve intimacy with another person until you have a clear understanding of the factors that contribute to your irrational thinking. It is important to develop a balance between separating from and attaching yourself to others. Many of the behavioral expectations listed in the previous developmental stages cover issues of independence and dependency. You can utilize the previous behavioral expectations as a guide to demonstrate love, respect, and honesty.

In this developmental stage, you will also need to take the additional step of reflecting on how well you met the behavioral expectations in each of the previous developmental stages. You will not recall the first stage, so begin with the second. As you go through each of the stages and evaluate your interactions with parents and other significant persons in your life, you will need to use the behavioral expectations as a guide. This can be a painful process for those who suffered many hurts throughout their childhood. This will help you to identify specific instances from the past that have contributed to your present negative thoughts, feelings, and behaviors. You can develop a time line by keeping a journal that contains the positive and negative memories of each year of your childhood that you can remember. This journal needs to include significant events that you experienced with another person. This journal will include your specific thoughts, feelings, and behaviors—as well as the behaviors of the other person—during these positive and negative encounters.

Did people significant to you in your childhood demonstrate love, respect, and honesty as depicted in the behavioral expectations? What did you consider to be loving, respectful, and honest from these individuals? How are you presently demonstrating love, respect, and honesty? Does your behavior demonstrate love, respect, and honesty based upon the expectations outlined in the developmental stages? There are many people that do not demonstrate love, respect, and honesty on a consistent basis. This does not mean that they are bad people or that they do not want to emulate these qualities.

Due to their irrational thoughts about life circumstances, they fail to shift their focus from them to the other person. They become self-absorbed in their needs brought about by irrational thoughts causing them to act in unloving, disrespectful and dishonest ways with the other person in their relationship. The most rational people also fail to demonstrate these virtues from time to time. Their ability to atone for these times are what demonstrate their rational approach to maintaining a positive relationship with another person.

Once this person has been able to evaluate how his or her encounters have influenced his or her perception of morality, he or she will need to create his or her own strategy to incorporate behaviors in his or her life that depict love, respect, and honesty. The behavioral list developed from these virtues does not have to include every behavioral expectation listed in this chapter. This person will also need to develop boundaries that are appropriate with the persons that he or she had considered close in his or her life up to this point. This does not mean that this person should stop having contact with persons that have been close to him or her. Once a person understands these virtues, he or she can determine whether to pursue a close relationship based upon the other person's ability to show these virtues and atone in genuine ways.

As mentioned, a relationship can be distanced without cutting ties with another person.

STAGE 7: PRODUCTIVITY VS. STAGNATION

In the middle-age stage of life, people become more aware of their eventual death. Their core struggle is between productivity and stagnation. Failure to reach their dreams can cause great pain in this stage. Therefore, the way in which you measure your productivity will determine your success in this stage. How do you measure your productivity or success? How does this measure impact your demonstration of love, respect, and honesty? Many people in this stage gauge their productivity by morally relativistic standards. They look at how society measures productivity. If you measure your productivity by symbols of success such as wealth, you will focus your efforts on the pursuit of those symbols. Along the way you may have to make sacrifices in other areas, including time away from the other person in your relationship. Wealth and other typical symbols of productivity are worthwhile pursuits, as long as you do not define your worth and value by your attainment of them.

In this stage of development, people compare their self-potential to their present achievements. Take time to identify personal growth opportunities along with your new life experiences. Focus on your ability to meet new people, participate in new activities, and learn new skills, which will help you to reach this potential. People in this stage also want to achieve self-acceptance. In order to do this, you must be able to develop realistic goals in life.

Also in this stage, your primary focus will be on the virtue of respect. You will need to continue to demonstrate unconditional acts of love, but you will not need to develop any additional behavioral expectations for love. Also in this stage you will focus on valuing yourself.

RESPECT

To demonstrate respect in this stage of development, you will need to develop behavioral expectations that depict your self-respect. Take time to find out what you like and dislike about yourself. What might you want to change about yourself? Will making these changes improve your self-acceptance? This is something you will need to give much thought to. In your daily evaluation, identify the specific qualities that you acquired in your attempts to meet your personal goals. Then, identify ways in which you will make the changes necessary to reach your self-potential. Those changes could include meeting new people, developing new activities, and learning new skills. You will show respect for the other person in your relationships when you ask for his opinion on how you can reach this level of productivity while still maintaining love, respect, and honesty in the relationship.

What do you like about yourself? What makes you feel happy and worthwhile? What would you be doing differently in order to feel a sense of personal achievement? Many people feel inadequate and stagnant during their middle years of life. This midlife crisis causes them to act in unloving, disrespectful, and dishonest ways. Many people conclude that they need a new relationship, a sports car, and a return to their adolescence. They do not accurately assess what they really need. Instead, they direct themselves to what they think that they want. Their ideas usually stem from the social customs presented today. Unless they find ways to feel adequate and productive, they become more self-absorbed and less virtuous. This is disrespectful to those with whom they already share relationships.

HONESTY

As you truthfully evaluate your willingness to make the changes to reach your higher potential, you are demonstrating honesty. Whenever you pursue a want or a need, you run the risk of recklessly abandoning the virtues discussed in this chapter. People who experience wants and needs can develop irrational thought patterns if they do not participate in activities that force them to consider and act on others' wants or needs. You must be willing to accept honest feedback concerning your hurtful behavior from the other person in your relationship. If you become self-absorbed, you will need to atone for the hurt this causes. You will also need to find ways to develop qualities that move you toward your self-potential while still demonstrating love, respect, and honesty. The art of negotiation and problem resolution are very important during this developmental stage.

STAGE 8: INTEGRITY VS. DESPAIR

The last developmental stage is late adulthood. The goal of this stage is to leave one's life with few regrets. The core struggle is between integrity and despair. In this stage of life you must be able to utilize your rational thinking and spirituality in order to maintain your integrity during the final years of life. You must be able to repair the hurt in your significant relationships in order to leave life with few regrets. Without the stress of children, work, or other daily commitments, you have a great opportunity to give back to others in your relationships by following the virtues described throughout this chapter. You can choose from the list of behavioral expectations and atoning strategies from each developmental stage. You could even serve as a role model for others, helping children, adolescents, and adults to meet their developmental milestones by encouraging them to adopt this type of virtue system in their lives. The elderly should not wait for a knock on their door to demonstrate virtuous behavior. They need to take the initiative to promote their wealth of knowledge and experience and show that they find value in those who are younger than they are. This is not a time for older people to be self-absorbed with thoughts of their dying or their medical conditions.

THE SYSTEM IN ACTION

As you read through the behavioral expectations from each of the developmental stages, you were introduced to behaviors that will put a positive spin on your approach to your relationship with another person. Through virtuous acts, you will ground yourself in the here and now. Past or future worries will flee when you demonstrate virtuous behavior, because your focus will have shifted. Additionally, you will learn to deal with conflict in a relationship by developing problem-solving skills. To maintain a rational mindset that will ultimately improve your relationship, you will need to make a concerted effort to perform the behavioral expectations that you choose to implement. You do not need to decide on your own what behavioral expectations to perform. You will experience better results if you allow a person close to you to help you make these choices. It is important to recognize that you may not possess the insight necessary to assess in what areas you are falling short of the mark.

You will need to set up a time each day when you will evaluate your performance of the behaviors you have decided to incorporate in your life. You will not always meet the expectations. However, your willingness to take responsibility for those times when you do fail to meet expectations will demonstrate your sincerity. If you find that you are failing to meet expectations on a consistent basis, you will need to evaluate whether your list of expectations is too extensive. You will need to negotiate this with the other person in your relationship. You should not wait too long to do this, or you will give the impression that you are not willing to repair the relationship. The atonement process needs to include your discussion of the success or difficulties experienced each day in performing acts of love, respect, and honesty.

BENEFIT 1: CLEAR GUIDELINES FOR BEHAVIOR

How can this system benefit you? By defining specific behaviors regarding your interactions each day, you will for the first time have clear guidelines. Many people fear what is unknown to them. Thus, when people do not have a clear picture of what is expected of them in a relationship, many of those relationships begin to fall apart. The sign that a relationship is spiraling downward is when communication ceases to be clear and effective. Without developing expectations grounded in virtues with an atoning process, you may create expectations that are unrealistic and irrational for the relationship. Maybe you expect or are expected to make enough money to purchase better things. Maybe you want the other person in your relationship to take sole responsibility for the household or childcare needs. Maybe you want to get drunk or high each day and not be criticized for your behavior. Maybe you want to have more than one intimate relationship that is sexual. The list of irrational expectations can go on and on. When a person decides to base his expectations on himself and on quick, "feel good" solutions, he will negatively impact the other person in his relationship. Where have you derived the expectations for your behavior?

BENEFIT 2: SKILLS FOR MATURITY

Another benefit that you will experience by following the behavioral expectations in this chapter is that you will gain skills to be a mature adult. There are not many road maps to adulthood. During their adolescence, many people do not gain the skills they need in order to be responsible and virtuous. In fact, many adolescents are given a moratorium from responsibility that lasts throughout their adolescent stage of development. Adolescents are not meeting the milestones mentioned in this chapter. They become ill-prepared to enter adulthood and meet the challenges of each relationship in the multiple roles they assume. Do you know of any adults that remind you of an adolescent? You will not have to look far to see adults acting as juveniles. Parents have assaulted other parents at their children's baseball game over a call from an umpire. "Adults" have tailgated or pulled right in front of vehicles due to their anger. So-called adults have resorted to verbal threats and physical attacks at work, at home, and in the community as ways to manage conflict.

What causes you to become verbally or physically aggressive? Throughout this book, you have read about factors that contribute to irrational thoughts. More adults are in crises today because they have not developed ways to cope with their stress. They have not learned how to behave with other people during times of peaceful coexistence and conflict. Schools, families, and community services are no longer teaching these relationship skills. This book is a guide that will help you in your relationships, especially when you need to repair a damaged one.

It will not be easy to shift to a more rational approach in how you think, feel, and behave; indeed, it will take practice. When you evaluate your past behavior, you may not want to accept the truth about the hurt you have caused. You may not want to face your present pattern of hurting others. This will take time to process and accept. In the meantime, you will need to honestly evaluate your behavior each day and recognize when you do and do not show virtuous behavior. If you find that you are not showing the behaviors that you choose to incorporate in your relationship, then you will need to take ownership for this and atone if you are going to repair the relationship. Do not be discouraged if you do not understand the virtues described in the context presented. Society does not depict love, respect, and honesty as outlined in this chapter. You will need to reflect on these virtues and plan ways to make them part of your daily presentation to the other person in your relationship. Once you can connect your use of these virtues to the improvements in your relationship, you will begin to understand the value of this system.

FOUR

SPIRITUALITY FOR ADULTS IN CRISIS

You have gained some insights into how you may be hurting the other person in your relationship. This may alarm you and cause you to put up defenses or try to rationalize your behavior. These reactions are psychological forces that go to work when you feel emotionally exposed and vulnerable. You will want to deny that you are the culprit. You may struggle to come to terms with this. Do not be alarmed if you feel angry or frustrated. Your new insights are not the only reasons why you may feel a sense of crisis. You have spent much of your life engaged in thought processes that were negative and reactive. You were exposed to factors throughout your life that reinforced your negative views on life. Due to your inability to rationally process situations that you encountered in each relationship along the way, you most likely have not met milestones in your developmental stages. This has posed challenges for you. You will need to practice the relationship skills outlined for each developmental stage that you have not met.

Have you been afforded opportunities to make independent decisions or test your morality? Many people have limited experiences with other people, places, or things. Can you base your outlook and decisions concerning relationships on your experiences?

To enhance your relationship skills, you need to gain more insight into the human condition. You now possess a structured outline as to how you can begin to relate to each person you come in contact with. You will need to show your talents and abilities to others and have them do the same to you.

Adults need to feel productive and leave behind few regrets. You may feel very dependent upon others, have no real sense of your morality, and feel very stagnant in your life. Your relationships up to this point have not been grounded in love, respect, and honesty. Your irrational thoughts will be hard to change because your instincts will be to look at the negative aspects of your relationship when a conflict arises. You will need to trust this new virtue/atonement process and stick to it each day.

You will need to evaluate how the stress and barriers in your life impact your thoughts, feelings, and behavior. You cannot use any of these life situations to excuse the hurt that you cause another person. Your tendency to view stressful situations in irrational ways will be a constant struggle for you. You will need to understand what contributes to your stress and learn how your body signals stress. Once you develop the ability to recognize stress, you can put safeguards in place to work through the stressful event without acting in ways that hurt another person. The key will be to remember to communicate in ways that emulate love, respect, and honesty. When you fall short of the mark, your atoning behavior will help to repair the hurt that you cause in your irrational state.

What causes you to experience stress? What are the physical and emotional signs that show that you are experiencing stress? Many people have learned to adapt to higher levels of stress and do not understand the signals their bodies are sending. Laptops, cellular phones, and other technologically advanced equipment have led to less down time for people. They end up pushing themselves to their limits each day and develop more irrational approaches to counteract the physical and emotional results of stress. Caffeine, anti-anxiety drugs, antidepressants, illicit drugs, and other artificial performance-enhancing substances are in the hands of more people today than ever before. These substances provide users with a false sense of emotional security. Are you becoming numb to the chaos around you? In order for you to gain the ability to think rationally, you will need to be able to identify signals of stress from your body and your emotions and to react to these signals in rational, healthy ways.

TAKE INVENTORY

Initially, the best way to identify your signals of stress is to conduct a "body and emotion inventory" while you are under stressful conditions. Prior to this inventory, you will need to determine if you are under stress by how positive or negative your outlook is on any given day. When you find that you are having a difficult time discerning any positive characteristics in the events, people, or places with which you are involved, you can be assured that you are under stressful conditions. What changes have occurred to your physical body during this stressful event? Do certain parts of your body feel tense, sore, or warm? Do you suffer stomachaches or feel shaky at all? Everyone's reaction to stress is unique. Find out what bodily signals relate to you, and then write them down. You may discover that these signals are occurring daily and correspond with your negative outlook on situations and your relationship.

Do the same kind of inventory on your emotions during a

stressful time. What are you feeling at that time? Most likely you are experiencing negative emotions such as frustration, anger, helplessness, or sadness. Once you have developed your lists for your body and emotional signals of stress, you will need to remind yourself to evaluate these signals throughout your day. There is a correlation between high levels of stress and increased irrational thinking.

MANAGE STRESS IN HEALTHY WAYS

The next step is to develop healthy ways to manage your stress. You do not want to mask how your body and emotions respond to stress. You need to feel stress as it occurs, so that you can make immediate adjustments to how you are thinking, feeling, and behaving in order to reduce your stress levels. When you notice a signal of stress, you should have a coping strategy in place. This will help you to work through the trigger to your stress in a rational manner. This chapter will include ten reflections that can help you to cope with stress by changing your irrational thoughts to rational ones. Your ability to recognize stress and to keep a proper perspective on life will also help you to focus your priorities on love, respect, and honesty toward another person. Until a successful stress-management approach is implemented, you will experience difficulties generalizing the virtues outlined in this book.

MAINTAIN REALISTIC EXPECTATIONS

Another key to your success with the implementation of this virtue/atonement system is for you to maintain realistic expectations regarding your success. Do not pressure yourself or the other person in your relationship to adopt this new behavioral approach without problems. Expectations that are too high or too low will not be realistic. Refrain from making personal attacks on the other person, and keep communication specific to the behavioral expectations that you both develop in the three virtue categories. Do not allow morally relativistic thinking to influence the behaviors and feelings that you bring to your relationship. Money, prestige, and instant gratification are some of the societal symbols that can lead to hurt in any relationship. You can pursue some of these symbols and still maintain a healthy relationship as long as your journey involves a commitment to moral absolutes and atonement.

DEVELOP A PERSONAL SPIRITUALITY

In order to manage your irrational thoughts and hurtful behavior during your transition time, you will need to develop ways to process your daily thoughts, feelings, and behavior in private ways. This is not to replace your daily evaluation of your behavior with the other person in your relationship. Rather, this needs to be a separate time for you to reflect and ask yourself some questions. The more time you spend engaged in introspective activities, the more you will generalize ways to express love, respect, and honesty in your relationship. Then, the better you become at visualizing ways to depict these virtues, the more you will succeed in demonstrating them in real situations. Without developing your ability to think rationally, you will continue to see yourself and others through a negative lens. People who learn to cope well with stress can also maintain a good perspective on their lives through a spirituality derived from meditative practices. These activities have helped many people to remain grounded in the truth.

Spirituality is a concept that is confusing to many people. Many people confuse spirituality with religious practices. The practice of one's spirituality is very personal. Your ability to develop a spiritual side to your life will further reinforce the virtues outlined in this book. Gaining an appreciation for your life through seeing how your actions contribute to a higher good is the key to spirituality. People who are anxious, insecure, and fearful have not made it their practice to tap into their spiritual side. They perceive life only as a futile struggle, rather than seeing life as a challenge that is meaningful.

When you look realistically and rationally at your life, your time is a precious commodity. Those who have known you will judge how you have spent your time and what you have left as your legacy. The concept of death is frightening to those who lack spirituality. Self-indulgence and other morally relativistic behavior consume the thoughts of many people during their spare time when their only focus is on their irrational thoughts and their fears. They visualize bigger homes, better cars, more jewelry, or a better significant other. They grow to resent the current people and possessions they have due to this irrational pattern of thought. They fear that they will miss out on some sort of pleasure before their lives end. This serves only to reinforce their emptiness and fear.

There are many books and resources concerning meditation and spirituality. The key to spirituality is the discovery of what it means to be human. You are challenged to visualize how you can give something back to benefit another person through the acts of love, respect, and honesty that you have learned about in this book. You are also challenged to accept that there will be times when you fall short. The human condition involves the struggle to become a better person while understanding that there will be peaks and valleys along the way. Up to this point, you may have placed blame on others for their wrongdoing toward you and have continued to feel angry, insecure, and anxious. You must let go of these negative feelings and create a rational vision for your life. Have you made the statement that life is not fair? This may be true, but it does not justify the hurt that you may cause another person. What can you do to positively impact another person in an unfair world? This is a better question to address. Your pursuit of becoming less selfish is crucial in your practice of spirituality. Taking from others will not bring you the meaning and happiness that you are searching for.

Your daily thoughts and meditations can consist of how you can make contributions to your relationship. They should also include an examination of your interactions with others each day and how well that you demonstrated love, respect, and honesty. You can utilize your list of behavioral expectations as a guide in your daily meditations. The manner in which you meditate is up to you. You will need to find a means to isolate yourself from others during the times when you meditate. The hardest part of meditation is your ability to focus. This may take time to develop. You will want to divert your attention from your worries and other factors that contribute to your irrational thinking. Some people can focus on a meditative activity immediately. There are breathing exercises and ways you can position your body that may help you. Research this for yourself, and develop a system that allows you to relax and remain focused on the targeted thoughts of the day. You will need to start out with small steps in this process. With meditation, as with any new activity in which you engage, it will take time for your mind and body to adjust to this new skill. However, the more you practice the art of meditation, the better you will get.

You may want to start your daily meditations by reflecting your daily interactions and how you demonstrated virtuous behavior. Over time, you will be able to expand your meditative thoughts to images of a broader meaning that comes out of your contributions to the human condition. The goal of your meditations will be to connect your daily actions to a higher meaning in your life. This will help you to connect to your spiritual side. Are your actions providing a benefit to another person? How does this contribute to a higher good? Can you connect your actions to how you feel? Through quiet reflection time each day and by using the virtue format to reflect, you will be able to focus on how well you are engaging people and writing your legacy. If you were to pass away today, what would the people who know you say about you? If you could write an epitaph for your gravestone depicting the kind of person you are, what would you say? Are you avoiding people? Are you expecting others to satisfy your needs? You may be waiting for others to respect and love you instead of demonstrating these virtues on a daily basis. You may be thinking that others will seek you out and love you.

You need to meditate each day in order to regain a sense of reality and a proper perspective on what is important. Many times, life stresses will cause you to lose perspective, which in turn causes you to become irrational and mix up your priorities. Through a daily ritual that lasts at least 30 minutes each day, you can reflect on life and rediscover the truth about what is meaningful and what is not. Many people spend most of their day reflecting on meaningless information. This is information over which they have no control. Do you obsess over things you cannot control? Do these thoughts consume you and cause you to be distant or hurtful to the other person in your relationship? Once you maintain a daily meditation ritual, you will gain the ability to see beyond your daily hassles and focus on what you can do to improve your relationships and find greater meaning in your life.

For those of you who would like some initial thoughts on which to meditate, the remainder of this chapter contains a list of daily reflections. These reflections will target some of your irrational themes that you pick up from your daily experiences with other human beings. These reflections do not target just the virtues of love, respect, and honesty; they also target themes that you may face that cause you confusion or concern. These reflections can provide you with ways to see the truth about a relationship and how you can fight your tendency to look at situations in irrational ways. You may not gain a sense of spirituality right away during your daily reflections. However, as you begin to think more rationally and incorporate the virtues of love, respect, and honesty in your relationship, you will find your spirituality.

MEDITATIONS

MEDITATION 1: HOW YOU FEEL IS NOT NECESSARILY WHO YOU ARE

This daily thought is a great meditation for person who begins to associate his bad feelings with the type of person he is. Have you experienced hurt in your childhood? If you think that a bad feeling is a reflection of your personality, you are making this connection through irrational thoughts. Once you begin to see that your bad feelings are separate from your personality, you can begin to allow those bad feelings to exist and not be so inclined to look for quick fixes to feel good again. People are drawn to chemical substances or other instant pleasures because their irrational thoughts have given them bad feelings. During this meditation, reflect on the day's thoughts and actions that contributed to your feeling bad. Spend time looking at how you came to the conclusion that you are a bad person due to these feelings. Was this evaluation of your behavior based on how you demonstrated love, respect, and honesty?

Initially, you will associate your bad feelings with morally relative themes. Maybe you do not have a big house, a sports car, or the job that you want. Maybe you think your life has not measured up to what is depicted in romance novels or the movies. How will your pursuit of these symbols of happiness improve your relationship? Will you go from a bad person to a good person once you attain these status symbols? This meditation can help you to identify the source of your bad feelings. Allow yourself to feel bad, but also look at how this feeling has impacted your ability to demonstrate the virtues outlined in this book. Let this be a signal that you are not looking to an absolute morality to guide your relationship.

MEDITATION 2: HOW SOMEONE MAKES YOU FEEL IS NOT NECESSARILY WHO THEY ARE

This meditation is similar to the first. You are reflecting on how you evaluate other people with whom you come in contact. Many times people will share their views or provide feedback that may cause you to feel sad, happy, elated, or hurt. You may often make the mistake of evaluating others by the feelings they provoke within you. This can cause you to act in irrational ways based on irrational assumptions. On what are you basing your feelings when you interact with another person? When someone makes you feel good or bad, what did he do to provoke this feeling? Does this automatically make him a good or bad person? You may be surprised how many times you have dismissed a person in your life because of his honesty. The truth can hurt if you are not ready to accept it. You may have dismissed an honest, trusting relationship because your evaluation of that relationship was based on irrational thoughts. This meditation can help you to assess a person according to the virtue system outlined in this book. Think about what another person said to you and how the statement made you feel. On what did you base your conclusions about this person? If he was being honest and respectful, were you angry at the truth? Were you thinking other irrational thoughts? If you can answer these questions, you will get a clearer picture of what is making you feel the way you do. You might not like it when others make you accountable for your actions. Sometimes you simply may not like someone's communication style or way of life. It is important for you to remember that how a person makes you feel may not represent the type of person that he is. He may actually be a very honest, respectful, and loving person.

This is also true for those individuals who make you feel good. Look at why he is making you feel good. Is he being dishonest with you by telling you what you want to hear? Is he demonstrating respect and love to you? Would an alcoholic's best friend be someone who went out to a bar with him? How do you think this same person would react if you told him that he had a drinking problem? This meditation will challenge your irrational thinking and allow you to reflect on how the virtue system can guide you in a relationship.

MEDITATION 3: IF NO ONE GOT HURT, IT IS NOT A BIG DEAL

This meditation is good for those times when you have made mistakes that have impacted others in your life. Perfectionists put themselves through tremendous trials and tribulations when they make mistakes or fail at anything. If you are a perfectionist, this meditation will help you to gain perspective in life. If you were not dishonest, disrespectful, or unloving when you made your mistake, then you need to look at what is causing you to dwell on the mistake. How do you assess yourself when you make a mistake? What are your thoughts immediately after you make a mistake? Do you think negative thoughts such as "I am stupid" or "I'm worthless"? Your irrational expectation to be perfect only leads to more irrational thoughts when mistakes are made. Your irrational thoughts, in turn, lead to negative feelings that can cause you to hurt others. Some mistakes may lead to more severe consequences in life, such as a lost job or a change in majors in college. In the scheme of life, however, these consequences are not a big deal compared with how people conduct themselves as human beings. How you conduct yourself is the theme of this reflection. In the end, your legacy will be how you treated others, not the educational, vocational, or material symbols you possessed.

Meditation 4: Shut Your Mouth So You Have Time to Think

This is not only a daily reflection but also a skill to incorporate in an emotional situation. Sometimes a person will provoke strong positive or negative feelings in you. Because you have a tendency to think irrationally and respond from those thoughts, you will relate better to others if you take time to process information communicated to you before you communicate your response. This should be only those times when you become emotionally charged with either positive or negative feelings. This meditation requires that you imagine yourself in these situations and think about what you are observing in the person who is eliciting this response in you. It is far better to remain quiet during these times than to respond in a way that causes you to become too vulnerable or to act in verbally aggressive ways. Is the other person demonstrating respect, honesty, and love toward you? If he is, then his message is grounded in truth and can be trusted. If the message is not grounded in truth, you will need to communicate this in an assertive way that is not hurtful.

To practice assertiveness, meditate on objective responses to the person who is eliciting your strong emotion. The response should include statements that are respectful and honest and demonstrate that you are in control of your thoughts, feelings, and behaviors. The practice of "I statements" is a good meditation to reflect upon each day. (The eighth meditation will discuss the use of "I statements" in more detail. See below.) Information communicated to you is only as powerful as you make it. You can make the sender's message more powerful if you respond in irrational ways. When someone sends you a message that elicits irrational responses such as name-calling or excuses, you have empowered his message. If instead you point out how disrespectful, dishonest, or unloving the message is, you have made the information provided by the other person powerless, while your message becomes very powerful. This is most effective when you communicate this in respectful, honest, and loving ways. This also rings true only if the other person's message was disrespectful, unloving, or dishonest. If he is telling you the truth about your behavior, you will need to take responsibility for your actions. Practicing this reflection will help you to develop a rational approach to communication and positive ways to manage your strong emotions.

MEDITATION 5: ENCOURAGE HOPE

This is a meditation that can help you to shift from pessimism to optimism. Many people are feeling as though there is no hope in their lives. In every type of relationship you are involved with, you will serve each person well by promoting hope. Meditate on how you can give hope to others. This book has listed many ways in which you can demonstrate virtues. Visualize ways in which you can share kind words and acknowledge the uniqueness of a person in your life. Visualize the response that you will elicit from this person when you take the time to value him as though he was the most important person in the world to you. It takes only one person to show an act of love or respect to help someone see the world a different way.

Meditation 6: Regain Your Focus When You Are Overwhelmed

This meditation involves your finding a way to ground yourself, or stabilize yourself, when you find yourself gasping for air. This relates to the earlier discussion regarding the ability to manage your stress. People, places, and things may elicit negative emotions that cause you extreme emotional distress. The simple act of breathing is very calming and will help you to shift your focus to the here and now. Many meditations and relaxation techniques utilize breathing exercises to achieve a meditative or relaxing state. You may lose your breath some days when you are faced with the challenges of family, work, and community and all the relationships that go along with these environments.

In what other ways can you ground yourself when you feel overwhelmed? Because of your emotional state, you may not always have the ability to ground yourself. You may need to develop a grounding technique that is easier to incorporate when you are under extreme duress and are experiencing very irrational thoughts. You will need to assess which of your five senses is the most grounding for you. Certain smells, touches, sights, sounds, and tastes can help you to redirect your focus on a sensation that will bring you back to a more rational state. Holding objects, eating candy, looking at pictures, smelling aromas, and listening to certain sounds are ways in which you can achieve a grounded state. When you discover what sensation helps you to focus, you can use this to start each meditation. You can also have this sensation located in the various places where you may encounter stress. You may even be able to keep an object with you at all times. Radios, candy, scented objects, stress-relieving objects, pictures, and other grounding sensations are portable. After you have established a means to regain your focus, you will be better able to evaluate your relationship within the virtues of love, respect, and honesty.

MEDITATION 7: WHY DO I FEEL PRESSURED?

As you take time to reflect on the internal and external conflicts that you encounter, you need to ask yourself the question, "Why do I feel pressured?" This meditation involves your ability to either process a current problem that you encountered in a relationship or to visualize a potential problem that you may encounter. What steps would you take to resolve the problem? What criteria would you use to determine the source of the problem? As you develop a better understanding of the virtues outlined in this book, you will be better equipped to recognize the hurt that you cause in the relationship. During times when you visualize potential conflicts, practice your approach to atoning for your actions. See the other person's verbal and physical response to your recognition of a hurt that you caused him. Visualize his change in demeanor from sadness or disgust to attentiveness and hopefulness. See his eyes connect with your own while you demonstrate your sorrow and feel the positive reconnection that you make with this person.

MEDITATION 8: MAKE "I STATEMENTS"

The most effective way to communicate to another person is by taking responsibility for how you think, feel, and behave. This meditation involves your assessment of how well you took ownership for your thoughts, feelings, and actions while communicating to another person. Did you blame him or her for your thoughts, feelings, and actions? By meditating on how you can assert your views while taking ownership for your thoughts, feelings, and behaviors, you can begin to develop a dialogue that will get the attention of those you engage.

Visualize how you would communicate to someone using the format for "I statements." You may find this difficult to do, or you may think it is silly. However, as you become better at this type of communication, you will discover its effectiveness. Saying, "I became mad because I did not appreciate when you called me a pushover" is a better way to communicate than saying, "You are an idiot." The key to this skill is not to blame others for how you think, feel, and act and not to make personal attacks. This does not mean that you cannot identify another's behavior that brought about your thought, feeling, or behavior. The key is not to blame his behavior for your response. You chose to feel, think, and act in the way you did. This may sound similar, but it has a better impact on the receiver of this message.

This style of communication will help you to identify specific behaviors that contribute to your feelings. This will force you to think in a rational way. Your tendency will be to blame another person for your negative feelings, when in fact his or her actions did not warrant this type of response from you. By following the format for an "I statement," you will be forced to compare your feelings to specific actions by the other person. You may think twice before making statements like, "I become so angry when you ask me to spend time with you" or "I become so angry because you do not want me to drink alcohol." "I statements" are a good way for you to gauge if the statement should be made or not. Reflect on those times when you have been angry. What did the other person do to make you choose to be angry? Did he want your attention or tell you the truth about how unloving, disrespectful, or dishonest you are? This type of processing will help you to look at the situation in a rational way. When in doubt, follow the fourth meditation.

This skill will take practice and can be done each day in a meditation where you visualize conversations you have with others. This method also is instrumental in communicating positive sentiments. "You make me happy" does not communicate the message as effective as "I feel happy because I enjoy your company and the way you value my opinion." By communicating sentiments of love, respect, and honesty in the form of an "I statement," you will catch the other person's attention and discover how powerful and meaningful communication really is.

MEDITATION 9: LOOK TO THE GOOD OF OTHERS

This reflection asks you to assess the conditions that you are placing on another person each day. Your irrationality is directly correlated to the expectations that you place on others. The higher your expectations, the more negative your outlook will become when the person falls short of the mark. This is not to suggest that you should not place expectations on your relationship. However, the expectation must match the type of closeness of the relationship and be based on the virtues of love, honesty, and respect. You may first need to learn about trust and boundaries as outlined in the previous chapter. Do you tend to raise your expectations of everyone you have a relationship with, resulting in your general negativity toward people? You will need to meditate on the good that you see in people you deal with. Do not let your irrational thoughts cloud your ability to see the good in others.

On days when you feel that another person is less than worthy of any praise, you may need to force yourself to meditate on the good in that person. Your ability to do this will help you to regain some rationality regarding the actual truth about this person and gain a positive perspective on the problem. For example, someone may have wrecked your car, ruined your shirt in the laundry, or spilled a staining beverage on the carpet. Does this make the other person bad? If you cannot find any good in a certain person, you may need to break ties with him or minimize your contact; otherwise, your response to this person will be only negative and hurtful. You must leave room for people to fall short of your expectations from time to time, and allow the atonement process to be a vehicle to "right a wrong." Making up is such a wonderful experience and speaks volumes for the effectiveness of the acts of atonement and forgiveness.

Meditation 10: What Will Others Say about You When You Are Gone?

It is never too late to write a better script for your relationship. This last reflection is to be used once you have developed a better understanding of the virtues/atonement process and have demonstrated the ability to recognize the hurt that you are causing in your relationship. You may be afraid to ask the other person in your relationship the above question. You may not be afforded the chance to change the perceptions of some of the people you have hurt in your life; maybe they refuse to forgive your actions. This does not mean that you cannot use your unique qualities to benefit other people.

What abilities and attributes do you possess that would provide a benefit to another person? Picture yourself giving a part of you to another person and the reaction of the other person. In your meditation, visualize that you gave to this other person without condition—other than your seeing his positive response. Imagine how this person would interact with others in your absence. Visualize that he was uplifted by your contact and is now able to use his own attributes to benefit someone else. Many people who lack spirituality do not believe that they can make a difference in another person's life; they do not understand how this can spread out to positively impact many other people. Your negative or positive actions toward another person can stay embedded in that person's memory for the rest of his life. Do you remember who picked on you as a child? Do you remember an act of kindness by someone when you were a child? Are you beginning to see how important your actions are to the other people in your life?

As you utilize your talents in ways that demonstrate love, respect, and honesty toward another person, you will begin to rewrite your life's script. As you demonstrate these virtues in each of your relationships, you will touch the hearts of many and may never really come to understand the impact that you made in each of their lives. Once you begin to focus on your ability to give back to society, you will find meaning in your relationships.

The person in your relationship will be the beneficiary of your selflessness.

During your discovery of the truth and your daily reflections, you may feel strong emotions surface. You may need to let go of your own hurtful past and use the act of forgiveness as a major part of your recovery. This will help you to channel your passion and energies on demonstrating your love, honesty, and respect for human beings.

Remember to allow yourself and others to make mistakes. Saying that you are sorry or having someone else do this is a very precious moment and does so much to heal the soul. Do not place conditions on people in order for you to act in honest, loving, and respectful ways. Through your daily reflections and evaluations of virtuous behavioral expectations, you can begin to set a course to repair your relationship. When you take your last breath on this earth, you do not want to have regrets and you will want to leave a positive legacy.

Lee Ann Womak's song, "I Hope You Dance," contains the positive messages and perspectives on life that are appropriate to reflect upon in your new approach to each relationship that you encounter in your new journey.

> I hope you never lose your sense of wonder,
> You get your fill to eat but always keep that hunger,
> May you never take one single breath for granted,
> God forbid love ever leave you empty-handed,
> I hope you still feel small when you stand beside the ocean,
> Whenever one door closes I hope one more opens,
> Promise me that you'll give faith a fighting chance,
> And when you get the choice to sit it out or dance,

I hope you dance… I hope you dance.

I hope you never fear those mountains in the distance,

Never settle for the path of least resistance,

Livin' might mean takin' chances but they're worth takin',

Lovin' might be a mistake but it's worth makin'.

Don't let some hell-bent heart leave you bitter,

When you come close to sellin' out reconsider,

Give the heavens above more than just a passing glance,

And when you get the choice to sit it out or dance,

I hope you dance… I hope you dance.

I hope you dance… I hope you dance.

(Time is a wheel in constant motion always rolling us along, Tell me who wants to look back on their years and wonder where those years have gone.)

I hope you still feel small when you stand beside the ocean,

Whenever one door closes I hope one more opens,

Promise me that you'll give faith a fighting chance,

And when you get the choice to sit it out or dance,

Dance… I hope you dance.

I hope you dance… I hope you dance.

I hope you dance… I hope you dance.

(Time is a wheel in constant motion always rolling us along, Tell me who wants to look back on their years and wonder where those years have gone.)

BIBLIOGRAPHY

American Psychiatric Association: *Diagnostic and Statistical Manual of Mental Disorders,* Fourth Edition. Washington, DC, American Psychiatric Association, 1994.

Bourne, Ph.D., Edmund J. *The Anxiety & Phobia Workbook.* Oakland, California: New Harbinger Publications, Inc., 1995.

Childhelp USA. At
http://www.childhelpusa.org/child/statistics.htm. *Child Abuse Statistics.* Childhelp, Inc., 2001.

Corey, Gerald and Corey, Marianne Schneider. *I Never Knew I Had a Choice, 5th Edition.* Pacific Grove California: Brooks/Cole Publishing Company, 1993.

Hostile Hallways: Bullying, Teasing, and Sexual Harrassment in School. 2001. http://www.aauw.org/2002/hostilebd.html
http://www.aauw.org/2002/hostilebd.html> .

Internet Crime Archives, *Mass Murderer Hit List: Intermittent Explosive Disorder.*
http://www.mayhem.net/Crime/intermittent.html.

Leo, John. Apologists for pedophilia. *U.S. News & World Report.* April 22, 2002.

Lumsden, Linda. Preventing Bullying. ERIC Clearinghouse on Educational Management, ERIC Digest 155, March 2002.

Miller, Angelyn. *The Enabler: When Helping Harms The Ones You Love.* New York: Ballantine Books, 1990.

Morissette, Alanis. *Jagged Little Pill: Perfect.* Hollywood California: Maverick Records, 1995.

Neufeldt, Victoria and Sparks, Andrew N. *Webster's New World Dictionary*. New York: Warner Books, 1990.

Nolin, Mary Joe and Davies, Elizabeth and Westat, Inc. *Student Victimization At School*. U.S. Department Of Education, National Center for Education Statistics, National Household Education Survey, 1993. http://nces.ed.gov/pubs/95204.html.

Resnick, David B. *Some Definitions and Key Ethics Concepts*, http://www.scicom.lth.se/fmet/ethics_03.html, 1997

Womak, Lee Ann. *I Hope You Dance: I Hope You Dance*. MCA Nashville: UMG Recordings, Inc., 2000.

Work and Family in America: Current Statistics, http://asweb.artsci.uc.edu/sociology/kunzctr/stats.htm, 1996

Youth Indicators 1996: *Trends in the Well-Being of American Youth*, U.S. Department Of Education, National Center for Education Statistics, Marriage and Divorce Ratios & Children of Single Parents, 1996. http://nces.ed.gov/pubs/yi/y9605a.html, http://nces.ed.gov/pubs/yi/y9611a.html.

ABOUT THE AUTHOR

For 20 years, Jay Krunszyinsky has provided service to others as a Juvenile Probation Officer, Case Manager, Therapist, Behavioral Specialist Consultant, and Administrator for several human services agencies. His clientele have included children, adolescents, and adults with issues that have included abuse, criminal involvement, drug & alcohol addiction, and psychiatric disorders. In 1983, Jay Krunszyinsky obtained his Bachelors of Science Degree in Business Administration. He later went on to obtain his Masters of Art Degree in Counseling in 1995. He is a Certified Psychiatric Rehabilitation Practitioner and Abuse Investigator for the state of Pennsylvania. He has helped individuals, couples, and families identify and work through hurt while promoting the development of positive relationship skills.